West of the Divide

West of the Divide

Voices from a
Ranch and a Reservation

JIM CARRIER

Fulcrum Publishing
Golden, Colorado

Library of Congress Cataloging-in-Publication Data

Carrier, Jim.
    West of the divide : voices from a ranch and a reservation
/ Jim Carrier.
        p.   cm.
    ISBN 1-55591-093-9
    1. Ranch life—Colorado. 2. Indians of North America—
Colorado—Social life and customs. 3. Colorado—Social life
and customs. 4. Spann family. 5. Knight family. 6. Ute
Mountain Indian Reservation. I. Title.
F781.3.C37   1992
978.8—dc20   91–58482
                                                       CIP

Printed in the United States of America

0   9   8   7   6   5   4   3   2   1

Fulcrum Publishing
350 Indiana Street, Suite 350
Golden, Colorado 80401

To the Knights and the Spanns

Contents

The Knights of Ute Mountain

Introduction

The idea for this book came from rambling. Moving from place to place in the West. For five years I have roamed the Rocky Mountains, scraping stories from the landscape, collecting lifeblood from people who lived there, scratching and peeking and moving on. The job was wonderful—like that of a miner on a mother lode who takes the biggest nuggets, the easiest to dig, and chases off to find another easy vein.

There is literary gold in the West, plenty of it, waiting to be unearthed. Stories of love and hate, heroism and greed, small tales and epics. But unlike minerals, stories of the West are forever being forged by the landscape, the hardship, the romance and myth: a regional magma that swirls elements and people into new creations, forcing them through faults to be picked at by the curious. A writer has only to throw some gravel in his pan and swish it around. The color, the value, settles out.

A claim can yield long-term wealth, too, if one chooses to stay and dig, to know one place well. But I didn't realize that when I started. Writing for a newspaper encourages drift. The maw of a daily paper sucks up ideas and stories, spits them out and sucks again. The "news," I'm afraid, is usually mined on the surface, the easy vein. Production is important. I was an editor once; the pressure is not to sell the paper, but to fill it.

At *The Denver Post*, I have been extraordinarily blessed with an assignment off this schedule—a commission, really, to take time, to drive the distances and dig a little deeper to bring the issues and flavor of the mountain West back to Colorado's Front Range, where *The Denver Post* does business. The result has been a rhythm more in sync with the source than the outlet: the seasons, the sowing, the life of a calf or grizzly cub, the migration of eagles and spawning of fish. The stories that rise from the cadence of the landscape and, in the daily diet of news, resonate with some basal truth.

Fortunately, I also had a form to display this wealth: the series. I had been at the *Post* but a year when we published the first long western series, "Autumn in the Rockies," over the period from the autumnal equinox to the winter solstice. It tracked winter south from the Canadian border down the spine of the Rockies to Mexico. But rather than being a natural history of coming cold, it focused on people and their movements, from an Indian rancher rounding up cows to Texas hunters gunning for elk, to migrant workers and snowbirds who moved as the geese do. It was movement, not unlike my own.

But even the migrant has a home, and I could not pass it without yearning. Thus evolved "Letters from Yellowstone," a series from the Park, a diary of a year, a devotional to an earthly rhythm, written in a log cabin. What ran through that series (later to become my first book) were not the critters so much as the characters, the humans who move through the Park and determine its destiny.

That project, which allowed me to know one place well, set the tone for the work that follows. I wanted to dig one vein again, both of place and people, to understand the impact of one on the other. On my beat, that could only mean the two classic characters of the West, the cowboy and the Indian. Both, at one time, wandered the West; a century ago they became "grounded" in their unique land-scapes of ranches and reservations. They are characters created by the big land and sky, so uniquely connected that it is impossible to think of the place without the people, and vice versa.

The Utes, like all Native Americans, came from Asia, but their functional history begins in Colorado, New Mexico and Utah. Their livelihood, their mythology, their character evolved from Eastern (oriental) genes planted in moun-tains and plains and desert. The Ute Mountain Utes are one of the few American tribes whose reservation, though di-minished in size, is really home.

The cowboy came much later but in a century fabricated from the land his own livelihood, dress, character and mythology. Many cowboys became ranchers or cattle-men—terms preferred by the ranch family you will meet. Their values were rooted occidentally.

The cultural clash that resulted is usually, and unfor-tunately, summed up in the phrase, "cowboys and Indians." The two families in this book are not in conflict except in a historical sense. They did not know each other. I chose them for their values, their understanding of their own histories, the clarity of their view, the depth of character and the variety of people in their families. It is not every family that can sustain a three-month interrogation. The Spanns and Knights could and did.

I found them by prospecting. I sampled their ore, assayed it and compared it to other families I visited on a long trip around Colorado. I guess you could say—if allowed to carry the metaphor to extremes—that I chewed on their metal and found it pure.

My gut played a role, too, as it did with both families. Their willingness to expose themselves grew from brief meetings of introduction, a handshake and, ultimately, unspoken trust. The stories were published without prior clearance. They read the pieces each morning like any other subscriber.

That weighed heavily on me. I wanted to remain a journalist, with an independent, critical view of their lives. But early on, I also accepted as my role that of a sympathetic channel through which these authentic, contemporary voices of the West could be heard. The result, I think, was an honest interplay.

I spent six months with these two families in 1989, three in the spring with the Spann family on their mountain ranch and three in the autumn with the Knights on the Ute Mountain Ute Reservation. I wrote three pieces a week for the front page of *The Denver Post*, working with editor Rick Farrant and managing editor Gay Cook. What follows is virtually unchanged from the newspaper series.

West of the Divide takes its name from the country beyond the mountains, west of the Continental Divide where both families live. It is a fabled land. Miners of various stripes have come and gone over the centuries to pick at precious material; I am only the latest. Because the Spanns and the Knights stayed and knew their places well, we all are enriched.

Jim Carrier
Denver, Colorado
September 1991

West of the Divide

The Spanns

of Gunnison

1

One Foot in the Eighteenth Century, One in the Twentieth

*I*n a broad bowl of milk-white, the bales of faded hay sat piled in the bottomland like giant Frosted Mini-Wheats. Sugar snow covered the stacks. To anyone but the ranch hands knee-deep in work, the western landscape was a midwinter idyll.

They wore bulky boots, choppers on their hands and thick brown overalls over jeans and long johns. They rode from stack to stack, hunched on a sled pulled by a Snowcat that churned through the snowfields. On top of each stack, they shoveled in the wind, clearing snow for spring when thaw would wet and ruin the feed.

"I'm glad you could come up now," said Ken Spann. "Because west of the Continental Divide, this is a big part of ranching—feeding."

His words hung as frost between us, and he looked at me from under the brim of a wool cap with earflaps pulled down around his jowls. The sun, the glare, the bitter air had turned his face the color of flank steak.

Spann, thirty-two, is vice-president of a ranch whose family roots go four generations deep in the Gunnison valley. His young son and daughter, living with their parents in a home built by their great-great-grandfather, made it five. The Spann cattle and brand are known statewide. So is their family: Grandma Lois, whose late husband, Virgil, built the Hereford herd; their son Lee and his wife, Polly, now in their fifties; and grandchildren Ken, Susan and Jan. With spouses, a couple of hired hands, teams of horses and computers, they raise beef cattle in country only God could have carved.

I went to Gunnison to spend three months with the Spanns. I wanted to learn the cattle business, to help with the springtime chores of calving, branding and trailing to pasture. I thought maybe I could even be a cowboy.

"We're not cowboys, we're ranchers," Ken said. He handed me a shovel.

Across the pasture near the Gunnison River sits the homestead where he was raised. Lee and Polly live there, in a low, white house under spruce trees. Around the house is a weathered collection of buildings, pens, corrals and calving sheds. Prominent among them is a little red barn where they keep their saddles, reins and horse blankets. Under the eves the family brand is painted in white, the T-open-A.

Last July, a Marlboro cigarette advertisement crew spotted the barn and shot a commercial in the Dutch doorway. The art director had posed the cowboy-models in "rancher" hats, with nice morning light streaming through hazed windows in the background. The cowboys smoked cigarettes stuck between mustachioed lips. Some months later, the barn and the butts showed up on the back of *Sports Illustrated.*

The Spanns were bemused by that tableau but also a little proud. For theirs is a land and life-style of envy for those who don't know about shoveling snow. Marlboro evokes such envy in me with nothing but a rope, a hat or a horse.

I am especially prone to such allure. I was born in the East and first heard "westerns" on the radio after school. I came of age when television cowboys filled the gray screen, and I still have a Hopalong Cassidy night-light—glass with Hoppy's picture, shaped like a gun in a holster. It used to keep me safe in the dark. Now in my bedroom it casts a romantic glow. I hoped while working on the Spann Ranch that I could get beyond that nostalgic glow. Any understanding of the West today requires that. And the Spanns expected that of me.

But I could see, from atop the haystacks, that it would not be easy. In the West, romance and reality come together on a ranch.

"Step over, Jammer. Step over." Ken Spann leaned hard against Jammer's huge rump and threw an armful of stiff leather onto his back. Jammer swung his head, chewed his oats and looked at Ken in the dark barn.

"This harness hasn't changed in 100 years," he said. "This harness on Jammer is probably older than us three together."

Deeper in the dark, Dan Zatterstrom lifted a collar on Jeepers, buckled the quarter straps to the polestrap and pushed the bridle through his teeth. The barn door swung open and the big Belgians lumbered out, their breath huffing in the chilled morning air. A second team, Jip and Jake, followed into a yard piled high with snow. They strained on the harness to the empty sleigh. Ken walked behind, straining back, and buckled them to the doubletrees.

"We don't have any other tractors," Ken said. "Them horses have got to do it."

Dan opened a barbed-wire gate, Ken yelled "hup" and the sleigh lurched forward with sixteen legs churning in the snow. Four heads nodded in rhythm. Two border collies sprang to life, Jessie riding and three-legged Tuck, her brother, hopping behind.

"We're not the Budweiser teamsters," said Ken. "We're just trying to get our work done."

Every winter morning from December to May, Ken and Dan feed 500 cows, each cow carrying an unborn calf. From the stacks of bales—forty-four wide, ninety-six long and nine high—they pile fifty bales at a time on the sleigh and ride through the herd, peeling green feed into the snow. Each cow eats thirty pounds a day. One bale feeds three cows. On colder mornings, the animals get an extra ration.

"Hup, Jip." Spann held four reins, one for each horse, but strung through rings tied to its partner. Pulling on one rein pulled bits in both. He swung the team tight to the right and backed them with difficulty into a stack of bales. "Little bit. Little bit." He tugged on the reins. "I'm warning. There's a skunk in that pile. I saw a dead one last year and did a Pete Rose into second base."

Spann is a man who thinks through ranching. His grammar sometimes belies his learning, a degree in animal science from Colorado State University and a law degree from the University of Colorado. He worked, while in school, for the conservative Mountain States Legal Foundation, a firm that once employed James Watt. But after law school in 1982 Ken chose to come back home, to fight the elements and to partner with his dad. By then Lee had given up the teams he had used all his life and had bought the Snowcat. Ken had to learn to be a teamster from the hooves up.

Jammers and Jeepers cost him $2,000, the other team $1,750. By comparison, parts and maintenance on the Snowcat were $1,200 per winter. A good team lasted fourteen or fifteen years. But even as Ken penciled his justification, I could see he also liked the sound, the smell, the tug of horses.

"You've got to have one foot in the eighteenth century and one foot in the twentieth. You save things that work."

The old way, though, required hand labor in the worst possible weather. Eight tons a day, all by hand, in cold or blow. It dipped to 42 degrees below zero last year in a country known for its numbing winters. A neighbor, Shirley Anders, measured 128 inches of snow in 1988.

"In snow, we just go ahead and feed," said Ken. "It's just miserable." He sank a hay hook into a bale. Throwing hay keeps him lean. He is slight, with cropped red hair and an auburn stubble on his face.

"Hup," he said, and the shaggy white feet stomped a new path through the snow. It was up to my thighs, and the big yellow hooves kicked it higher. The three-ton sleigh groaned with the weight. Dan rolled the hay off each side, collecting orange baler twine in one hand. The cattle swarmed in behind. I sat on a bale and took in the scenery. Ken handed me a hay hook.

His ranch is eighteen miles from Lee's and lies on the road to Crested Butte. The snow that falls on the ski area falls here also. The mountains erupt from the edge of the pastures: Round Mountain east, Crested Butte to the north, Flattop and Red to the west, all of them higher than 10,000 feet. Slumgullion Creek and Roaring Judy run from their flanks to empty into the East River, which runs by the ranch. Just down the road, the East and the Taylor join to form the Gunnison.

"Why it's certain-sure the greatest country that lies outdoors," said an early visitor to the Gunnison area. "It's as big as half a dozen of your States back East. It has the richest mines of gold and silver. It has hills of coal and forests of timber. It has kingdoms of grass for cattle, empires of valleys howling and weeping to be ploughed, and rivers just ready to strike. ... And scenery? Great Jupiter! There's just scenery till you can't rest." (Ernest

Ingersoll of the Hayden survey, quoted in
Duane Vandenbusche, *The Gunnison Country*
[Gunnison, CO: B&B Printers, 1980], p. 58.)

In 1899 a family of six brothers named Spann arrived
from Missouri. They were skinners for the mines and settled
along the East River. They cut out homesteads all around
Jack Howe's stage stop, halfway between Gunnison and
Crested Butte, an area now known as Jack's Cabin. They ran
water to their grass, cut hay in the summer and trailed cattle
up the steep slopes of the mountains around them. For 100
years the routine continued.

Ken lives in his great grandfather's house. He uses
the log barn that has been rolled beside it. And when he cuts
hay each August, he raises the sickles as they pass over the
old foundation of Jack's Cabin.

At 11:30 A.M. Dan opened the gate, and the horses
stomped into the yard, anxious to get to their own hay. They
stood steaming as the harnesses came off. Hoarfrost tinged
their winter coats.

Ken got a syringe for a sick heifer wheezing with
pneumonia in a calving shed. Her calf lay frozen in a corner,
aborted and dead. An animal, probably one of the dogs, had
chewed on the black carcass. Ken injected two shots of dark
antibiotic into the mother and invited me in for lunch.

Mary, his wife, was making onion soup. She sauteed
the onions and added wine and beef broth in a way that
made cooking seem second nature to her.

"There are not many young ranchers our age," she
said. "Most women work. They need the added income. I'm
not on the payroll, but I'm fairly well compensated. We do
what we want when we want."

Mary is short, with brown hair and a quick smile. She
was raised near Cortez on a farm and she knew Ken's sister
in 4-H. At CSU, she asked Ken out and they married July 1,

1979. Mary earned a degree to teach home economics, but she practices it instead. Laura, their first child, is three. Andy is two. As we talked, they ran by and she slowed them down.

Mary cooks on an electric stove. An old Majestic wood burner collects mail, and next to that sits a microwave. The old house has a new kitchen, a renovated coal furnace and is about to get a new bathroom.

In a cluttered office, Mary showed me the ranch computer and a program she wrote. It figured the hay ration for each of the cows, based on the weather, their weight and protein needs. When the temperature plunges, she gets a new printout and Ken throws out some extra bales. The computer also figures the ranch's books.

"Our life and work are pretty much the same," said Mary. "We don't feel like we have to get away from it all."

2

Life and Death on the All-night Shift

*L*ee Spann didn't look particularly happy—or warm. On horseback behind the bawling cattle, he cut a figure in his cowboy duster, like he'd been there before, many times.

"Are you looking forward to this?" I asked him.

"Not really," said Lee.

The spring Spann cattle drive was underway, with most of the family out on the road trying to steer 473 mama cows eighteen miles through Gunnison to warmer calving ground at Lee's place. The drive would take two days and it was starting on a downer, a blustery day with a wind from the north and signs of snow.

Polly had asked the local country radio station to announce the drive beginning at seven o'clock, but at eight, the traffic in front of Ken's was like any other winter day: vans and buses headed north for the ski resort at Crested Butte. We were headed south.

"Hut, hut," the men yelled. "Shhh. Shssss." Lee whistled at the red and white Herefords and the black baldies. He tipped his head into the wind. "Trade you for that coat," he said to me. I was wearing down from L. L. Bean, with coyote fur on the hood. I hollered, too, and tried my best to push the cattle onto the road. I was riding Jack, a black quarter horse who wanted to go.

Ken was on the highway trying to get the long trail started. But the first few cows, turned back by a skier's jeep, headed toward Crested Butte. Grandma Lois, who is eighty-one and was driving the rear flag car, stepped out and waved the cows back. It was a rickety start. A Pepsi truck, another jeep and a van went by, then the blue and white First Baptist church bus.

"There must be a harder way to do this, but I can't think of it," said Lee. Lee is the laconic president of Spann ranches, a man given to blunt pronouncements learned the hard way—outdoors. He learned at his father's side and now is learning to share that experience with his children.

"The first three miles are O.K.," he said. "It's the last three that get old."

When I had asked if I could wear heavy winter boots rather than cowboy boots in the narrow stirrups, Lee had replied: "It's better to have cold feet than stuck feet. That's how wrecks happen." "Wrecks" was a word he used a lot. He'd seen a number of them in his fifty-six years. One year on this cattle drive, the driver of a tractor-trailer load of steel ignored Mary and her red flag and rammed head-on into the cattle. Eight cows and calves were killed. The truck also just missed Mary, and the sheriff thought Lee was going to kill the driver.

One year a tourist got out of his car in the middle of the herd and began taking pictures, scattering cows in all directions. "All I could see were white faces coming at me," said Lee. "I knew there was something bad wrong. He called me a rude old-timer."

Within an hour the cattle were on the road and stretched three miles in uneven bunches. Polly drove the family car up front with a sign on the bumper: "Slow, Cattle Drive." Ken rode a horse behind her, to steer and brake the plodding line. I stayed at the tail. Lee and Susan's husband, Bill Rivale, moved up and down to unbunch the cows when they filled the road.

"You've got to pay attention all the time," said Ken. The 473 cows with calves were worth $820 apiece. He thought a moment. "Half a million dollars worth. This is our business." He pounded his saddlebag. "Our office."

I asked him about the wisdom of trailing that much wealth—the family jewels—through town and traffic. He figured aloud this time: You could put fifty-two head in a semi-load. That's eight loads. But it's like putting water balloons in a steel container. It would probably cost $1,500–$2,000 to haul by truck. It made sense to let the cows walk at their pace, three miles an hour.

Skiers and beer trucks inched through, some more impatient than others. When a car honked a bit too much, Lee hollered down from his saddle, "You're in an awful hurry." Under Colorado's open-range law, cows on the highway are a driver's liability.

An Alpine Express bus went by, filled with skiers in bright clothing. Kids waved. People smiled. "I want to get a cowboy," someone said and snapped my picture through the open window. I sat up taller in the saddle.

"One thing about skiing, there are more pretty girls going up and down this road," said Lee.

A week earlier Lee had watched "Lonesome Dove," the television series based on Larry McMurtry's book about a cattle drive from Texas to Montana.

"To drive cattle from Texas to Montana takes grit, just to think about it," Lee said. People in those days weren't as settled. "They'd move in, use it up and move on. That period has been romanticized. There was a lot of hardship. 'Lonesome Dove' showed some of that."

Just then, a black BMW with a cellular phone and Texas plates inched past. These days the only Texans driving north are skiers. A woman inside climbed through the sunroof to take a photo. The car was surrounded by cows' butts.

"There's only so much you can take a picture of back here," said Lee.

A light snow began to pepper our backs as we passed Jack's Cabin Cemetery. The wind groaned through its evergreens.

Dan Zadra, a Spann hand, arrived to take Bill's place. Bill had an anthropology test at Western State College. But when Dan mounted, the horse bucked him onto the asphalt. He went back for his cowboy boots, but it didn't help. The horse reared again and smashed his glasses against its neck. Dan then walked the horse, which was on tryout from a neighbor.

"I think we've tried him enough," said Lee.

The day ended as cold as it had begun, halfway to the ranch. The cattle spent the night in a pasture along the road. The next day, however, was sunny. We all shed a layer. Jan, sixteen and a high school junior, joined us, dressed in jeans and jean jacket. Her flaming red hair waved behind her when she galloped after a wandering cow.

"You trying to make a fashion statement or something?" giggled Susan, her older sister and a fashion designer. Susan had made her father's duster, but she wore overalls, the unisex uniform of a Gunnison winter. A scarf covered her red hair. "I'm just a hired hand," she said and drove off pulling the horse trailer.

At the edge of Gunnison, Ken turned the herd west on Spencer Street by a hardware store and past pastel homes in a subdivision. A few cows walked into a yard and began eating grass. I headed them off with Jack. We turned left on Elizabeth, rode past the A&W and reached, at last, the service road along U.S. 50.

By now my saddle was made of rocks, and everyone wanted to get home. The cattle wanted to graze in the ditch. We passed Lee's house and reached the pasture. As the cows filed through the gate, Ken and Polly counted them. The cattle fanned out and began grazing.

Across the wide field, I could see the haystack we had shoveled earlier. The snow was beginning to thin in wide swatches of greening grass. Water was running in small puddles. I pictured the scene in "Lonesome Dove" when the music swelled and the cows reached Montana at the end of the trail. It was a silly comparison.

The Spanns had slept in their own beds both nights of the drive. Before she joined us, Jan had sung at a school concert and Lee and Polly had attended. No one ate from a chuck wagon. I had dinner at Pizza Hut.

And within a week the calves would start dropping. For the Spanns the work was just beginning. So was my story.

The road to the Spann Ranch runs through land that men dreamed about when the West was young. All it took was a climb over the Continental Divide.

On the other side a promised land of mountains and meadows spread away from the Sawatch Range. The pioneers crossed at Cochetopa, Marshall, or as I did on U.S. 50, at Monarch Pass. The highway follows Agate Creek which spills into Tomichi Creek which wanders west through a wide lowland to the heart of Gunnison country. Known for its mining, it is also cattle country. Not good cattle land, Lee Spann will tell you, because of the winters. But a place where a man can make a living.

The first cows were government issue, to feed Ute Indians displaced by miners. The first rancher, in 1872, was Alonzo Hartman, hired to run the Indian agency herd. He built a small cattle empire at the point where the Tomichi flows into the Gunnison River, a place he called Dos Rios.

Hartman fed the miners and later put steers on the Rio Grande narrow gauge that climbed the Tomichi, crossed the Divide and unloaded at stockyards in Denver and Kansas City. Exactly ninety years later, Hartman's ranch became a golf course, surrounded by condominiums and upscale homes at Dos Rios, two miles west of the city of Gunnison. An old irrigation ditch still runs through the development, carrying water to one operating ranch. In the spring when the ditch is full, errant golf balls by the dozens wash into the pastures of the Spann spread.

It was spring when I arrived. A few brave golfers were swinging in parkas, and across the road the ranch was in full bloom with calving. I came to the Spanns' to study a modern cattle operation and to get at the chief source of western mythology—the ranch. I chose the Spanns after a long search, after finding that a "typical" ranch does not exist. There are corporate ranches, prairie ranches, bankrupt ranches, hobby ranches, yearling ranches, purebred ranches and desert ranches—all different. The family ranch is in decline in Colorado. Not so at the Spanns, with three generations still working their cattle, still successful.

Although the Spann Ranch is a bit too close to civilization for my romantic tastes—jets loaded with skiers roar out of Gunnison right over the calving barn—the proximity highlights a number of issues I wanted to write about: the pressures of development, tourism conflicts and water rights. Lee sits on the Colorado River Water Conservation District, and Ken files the ranch's objections to Front Range water projects.

But what attracted me most was the cast of characters, from Grandma Lois, the matriarch, to Manuel Castro, the *vaquero* from Mexico who worked for the family each summer. They were links to the past. Lois had been married to Virgil, whose father ran freight for the miners in 1899 and homesteaded. Virgil built the Hereford herd and passed it on to Lee before he died in 1983.

He also passed on a way of life, old corrals and granite blocks by many of the gates. Virgil had been a short man, which meant high stirrups on his horses. In his later years he hauled in blocks from a nearby quarry that had supplied stone for the state capitol. He set the blocks at strategic locations so that after closing a gate he could stand on the blocks to get on his horse. The blocks are still there.

Today, Lee runs the place, with droll humor or sharp commands. He demands work but outworks them all. He is a man, said his wife Polly, "whose motor runs better uphill." They run 1,400 head of cattle, 800 of them mother cows about to produce calves for midwestern feedlots and national meat markets.

They own 3,600 acres on four different ranches and they lease thousands more from the federal government—leases that date to 1927 when Virgil began building the place. Their core is the home ranch, 700 acres near Dos Rios. Virgil and Lois bought it in 1932. Ken lives halfway to Crested Butte on 600 acres homesteaded by his great grandfather. The biggest piece is the cow camp—2,000 acres of verdant pastureland just outside Crested Butte. It is 1,000 feet higher than the home ranch and a world apart (more snow) in spring. The fourth piece is a 300-acre farm in Delta, banana-belt country to the Spanns, where they winter their calves and raise some grain.

Shortly after I arrived, Lee drove me up the valley to Crested Butte to see the snow cover, still two feet deep, on the cow camp. "We'll need the Cat to get at that hay," he said. He spoke from beefy lips below a large nose, weathered raw like most of his face. Only his forehead, under a hat, was white.

We also looked at Ken's ranch, where frozen turf was beginning to show in long brown patches in the snow. Ken and Mary had moved to the home ranch for calving. They rented a condominium across the road on the golf course.

I moved there, too, a bit embarrassed that life on a ranch had come to this: a view of the front nine at Dos Rios Country Club. There would be no bunkhouse, no chinked log cabin. The sign by the microwave said, "Please help us maintain our vinyl by not wearing your golf shoes inside."

Ah well, in his later years, cattleman Virgil spent a lot of time in golf shoes. He wintered in Mesa, Arizona, but around calving time he would return to the ranch. As the weather improved, he would buy buckets of used golf balls from his grandkids, dipped out of the irrigation ditch that ran across the ranch. He would take them to Crested Butte, balance them on a tee and drive them into cow camp.

There isn't much work for a cowdog in spring. So Rascal and Lady do the greeting. They shoot off the porch when someone drives in. They round up pickups and stray dudes like me and tell the Spanns someone is coming. Rascal is an old, brown Australian shepherd who showed his front teeth but then slunk off. Lady, a black and white border collie, soon dropped her attack for a stick. The dogs, like the owners, are protective of the place.

It reminded me of watching *Shane*, the Alan Ladd movie based on the Jack Schaefer book. Dogs barked at strangers in the film as they rode through Joe Starret's gate. The Spanns have a gate, too, in a white board fence that surrounds their house. Their name is painted on a brown wood sign, which hangs on a chain beside the road. "Virgil and Lee Spann," it reads above the T-open-A brand. "Commercial Herefords."

The house is on the right, white with dark shutters. The silhouette of a horse and carriage is tacked to each shutter. As I approached, a brisk spring wind blew through spruce trees and the cottonwoods that line the drive. The wind came from the west, up the Gunnison Valley from Blue Mesa, where ice still covered most of the reservoir. The sage-covered hills to the north were bare except for long strips of snow in the draws and along Steer Gulch. The meadows between the hills and the house were covered with cattle.

Each morning the hands gather in the driveway by a red log garage with a Standard gas pump in front. The staging area for the day's work is filled with pickups, tractors, trailers, old barrels, a pile of batteries for electric fence and Lee's old Willys jeep with the doors hanging off and a box on the back for carrying calves or dogs or tools.

Bill Rivale, Susan's husband, was wearing his chaps, and as usual, his black cowboy hat. "I'm hot blooded," he said. Bill would be horseback, cutting pairs of cows and new calves. Manuel Castro wore insulated coveralls and a cap with earflaps. He nodded and went off to feed hay. Lee was in his winter clothes, too, a shredded jacket and overalls. His gold-rimmed glasses had turned dark and his gray hair curled out beneath his insulated hat.

"I'm not into wind," he said, gritting his teeth. He opened a gate and stalked up a lane of old logs, new timber and boards chewed thin by the horses. The lane was broken by an array of gates that swung with various degrees of difficulty. Lee was forever reminding people to close them. "Let those cows come to water," he said to Susan, who was nursing a calf and milking a heifer with a bloated udder.

"And don't forget to shut the gate," yelled Joe Starret to Joey, his son, in *Shane.* In that classic western, sodbuster Starret had carved a homestead from range run by the Riker brothers. Old man Riker wanted it back. "We made a range out of this," he said to the sodbuster. He showed his arm wounded by Indians. That seemed to be the history of the West: one group pushing on another. It was so with the Spanns.

"They fought the Indians and we fight the environmentalists," said Polly when I mentioned the film. I didn't know what she meant exactly, but I began to sense that stories on the ranch were timeworn. The Spanns met their adversaries head-on. I could see why they were protective.

As the wind picked up and signaled a coming front, a more immediate adversary appeared on the horizon: snow, darkness and the penchant for cows to drop their calves when things couldn't be worse.

Big, wet snowflakes drifted past the yard light as Susan emerged from the dark lane. She was wrapped against the night. The dogs were asleep. The only sound was the scuffing of our Sorels and the soft whisper of snow, which, in the hour since midnight, had piled an inch on the Willys.

Susan opened the canvas door, found the flashlight and read the note on the jeep's clipboard from Lee: "Susan—Raining but warm. No. 591 new calf just east of trees out from corral. 648 just calved. I gassed the jeep. Dad." She stepped on the starter, latched the dripping door and lumbered across the wood bridge into the middle meadow. Another calf-watch was underway at the Spann Ranch. From late March into May, the 800 cows give birth to calves fathered by bulls last July and August. "They never calf when its warm," said Lee, who has fifty years of calving behind him. "Oh, they do, but not like they do when it storms."

Susan swung a spotlight along the fences and beneath the cottonwoods where the cows had taken shelter. She drove close and pointed the light at eartags to read the numbers. "These babies are up and their mamas are licking them," she said.

The light stopped on a black cow standing over a brand new calf. It was a slurpy yellow mess. The big tongue lapped at the little body, tossing the calf's head as it tried to find up from down in a cold cruel world. "Good job, girl," Susan said softly. She wrote the eartag number on the clipboard and drove on. In a few minutes the calf's coat would be dry of its birthing fluids and fluffed up against the snow.

We bumped across a ditch and drove beside snow-banks piled by the Spanns to clear the meadow. A calf with a white face and a black spot on its eye lay on the snow. Susan stepped out and nudged it to grass. Its mama mooed, moved closer and licked it.

"I used to go with Dad at 6:00 A.M. before school," she said. Now twenty-six years old, she and older brother Ken take the night shifts. She calls Lee only for problems. "We lost one last night. Dad and I pulled it."

She has strong hands with dirt beneath her finger-nails. Her face is freckled, and her long red hair is parted in the middle and pulled back alongside her head in a tail. When she speaks to the calves, it is like a child to a doll. "Smart baby," she said at one point. Her light found a calf on the wrong side of a barbed wire. She pushed it back.

"Have you ever seen a calf born?" Susan turned to me. I couldn't remember if I had. She drove behind a fat black heifer on the ground. Her tail was raised and she shifted with labor. A gossamer balloon hung behind her. I could see yellow hooves and a tongue inside. The tongue moved. We watched as the head emerged, then the neck. The heifer shifted and looked around.

The placenta balloon swelled in size. Susan crept close to the heifer and with her finger popped it open, draining fluid and freeing the head. The eyes were wild, the tongue stuck out. The heifer saw us and stood up. The calf was out to its ribs and hung down below the tail. The heifer swung and the calf crashed out in a shower of blood and yellow fluid and after-birth. The heifer turned, sniffed at her baby and began to lick. The snowflakes touched and disappeared on its body.

Over the years the Spanns had raised their calf weights by using bigger bulls. That usually gave a two-year-old, first-time heifer trouble. Fifty percent of them need help to pull the calf free. A week earlier, a note from Ken told of a long night:

"1:45 A.M. 758 calved near drain ditch snowbank. Pulled 776 in field at 2:50. Hip locked pretty bad. May be a little dinged, lucky to be alive.

"3:00 A.M. 661 new, also 6109.

"3:15 new calf.

"3:30 cow unsettled at old bridge.

"4:05 heifers O.K. Happy Easter. Ken."

Susan thumbed through the old notes and wrote one of her own. "Old cows O.K.," she wrote at 3:00 A.M. "Several new babies. All O.K. Several on the other side of fence. We put back in. Suz." She parked the jeep by the gas pump and walked down the cottonwood lane, across the road to the log house to curl up beside her husband.

By 6:30 A.M., Lee was riding the field on horseback. The wind had picked up, and the changing barometer kept him busy. He drove a troubled heifer to a red "maternity" barn, where he talked in a whisper. "Old girl. You've got a nice baby there." He edged the cow into a stanchion, tied her nose and helped her calve. He was gentle and quiet. "How you treat them, they treat you."

That night at 1:30 A.M. I met Ken for his shift in the fields. We drove in his pickup, with floodlights on the cab and the Fred Sanders Interstate Trucking Show on the radio. "It's company, anyway." The wind had died and the snow had stopped. At 2:00 A.M., with flashlights in hand, we left the pickup and walked a heifer into the barn. Her back had been arched for an hour, and the feet showing beneath the tail had not moved. Ken popped the water bag, looped obstetric chains around each ankle and pulled. Then he attached the chain to a ratcheting calf-puller, a Y-shaped bar that braced against the heifer's thighs. Within minutes the calf was out.

Ken, too, talked quietly. Not about money, which each calf represented, but about its health and survival. In the pickup, he discussed economics of ranching. Each calf is a small future for the ranch. Each successful birth is money in the bank. But I never got the sense that he or Lee or Susan thought of profit when the calf hit the ground.

At 3:00 A.M., we walked another heifer into the barn and Ken handed me the chains. I stood behind her and reached into the warm, moist vulva. As Ken talked me through it, I pulled on each leg, feeling them give as the baby hips slipped past the pelvic bone.

"I used to love putting my hands in there on cold nights, to warm them up," Ken whispered.

The puller in place, I moved the bar with each contraction. The head popped free and I pumped the ratchet. The calf slipped out with a gush, and Ken caught her and laid her down. Her chest began to quiver and the nostrils flared. The tongue sucked at air. She was breathing. We lifted her into fresh straw in a pen and let her mother follow. She sniffed, then licked. The calf raised its wobbly head.

I wanted to watch this miracle unfold, one I had played a small part in. But Ken waved me toward the door. We had more cows to look at.

The baby calf wobbled in the straw beneath a black skin draped on its back. Its spindly legs poked through holes cut in the skin. And it tried, with Lee's help, to suck a young cow in the pen.

"Neither one knows what's happening," Lee whispered.

The heifer sniffed at the blood-smeared skin. She recognized her calf. She didn't know that her calf was dead and that its skin hid a substitute. The smell was right, so she let the orphan have its breakfast. Lee waved in silence to leave them alone. In a couple of days he would take the skin off, and a new cow-calf pair would return to the range.

On the Spann Ranch, each day is dotted with little acts of heroism. Saving calves, keeping them alive, playing

God with animal skins. But death gets its share, too. Jeepers, one of the ranch's big draft horses, died shortly after we photographed him pulling the hay sleigh through the snow. It may have been colic. He was worth $1,000. Five percent of the calves die at birth. Another 5 percent will die before they wean in the fall. That's eighty calves this year for the Spanns. At $500 apiece—their worth in the fall—the loss totals $40,000.

"Death is part of the business," said Lee. "It's the ones that get sick and die that bother me. It's our job to pick them up and doctor them."

The carcass of the skinned calf lay by the corral when I first arrived. The dogs picked at it. In a few days, a second calf was dragged there, one with a cleft palate that daughter Susan had nursed for a week. "Miracle," she had called it— until it died. All the hands walked by the spot where the bodies were piled—reminders of reality on a ranch. The Spanns don't like to find animals dead. They want to try, at least, to save them. Their hard-nosed business sense rode side by side with their joy for life.

One afternoon while moving cattle between pastures, I found a calf claimed by two cows. They each bawled, sniffed and doted over the newborn, just what you'd expect from a new mother. But somewhere in the herd of white faces another calf was going hungry. In a few days it would die. We rode at dusk to find it and failed. At 2:00 A.M., Ken succeeded.

Using a burlap sack to transfer the smell of the twice-claimed calf, the Spanns pulled another switcheroo and got the right calf with the right cow. "You hunt and hunt and hunt to find her," Lee said. "It's not the economics that's driving you."

He handed me a coffee can full of water mixed with antiseptic. "How are you at tying prolapses?" I balanced the can as he wheeled the Willys down the east fenceline to a cow lying on her side. Ken and Bill were there with their horses.

The cow was in pain. A bright-red blob of tissue, the size of a basketball, had pushed out from her insides. Her uterus was exposed and blood was spurting onto the ground.

Bill tied her feet and sat on her head as she struggled. Lee pulled his shirt off, washed his hands in the coffee can and knelt behind the cow to wash the exposed tissue. He began to push the mass inside her. Ken pushed too, and Lee's forearm disappeared. He slipped on the ground as the cow strained back. "Push my elbow," he told me. Six hands were not enough to squeeze the tissue into place.

"How's her eyes, Bill?" Lee said.

"Her nose is going white and yellow."

"She's in shock," said Ken.

The cow's legs quivered and Lee's whole arm went inside. Ken got a big needle and suture, dipped them in the coffee can and tried to puncture the tough skin as I held it. He ran for pliers in the jeep and made one hole before she shuddered.

"I think she's dead," said Bill.

"Her heart's still beating. I can feel it on my hand," said Lee.

She quivered again and lay still. We all stood up.

"The calf still in her?" I asked.

"Yeah," nodded Lee. They took out knives.

"You sure she's dead?"

They cut at the rib cage, slashing at the cowhide, through the meat and organs that spilled out. Ken reached in. "Here's a leg." He grabbed the uterus, a long gray bag, and cut it. Bill found the face just as Lee yanked the calf out and flopped her on the ground.

Her nose was white. She was dead, too.

We stood for a moment, nothing left to do. Someone said, "Well, we tried." Ken looked in the cow's ear. She was born in 1972 and had produced fifteen calves. She was an old cow. She had paid her way.

Lee and I went back to the house to wash for lunch. Blood covered his face, my face, our shirts, our arms, our pants.

"She bled to death, that's what I think," he said. "It's not her fault. It's mine. I let her go too long."

3

A Fashion Statement
and Vissi d'arte

*B*eneath the cattle chute, ten feet were visible: four big cloven hooves facing forward, four little ones facing backward, and angulated among them, a pair of turquoise Reeboks with raspberry trim.

Susan Rivale was at her post. "This is where I spend a lot of my time," she said, bent over a scrawny calf, trying to get it to suck from a cow's bloated udder. "I hate newly brought-in cows. Their bags are tight and sore, and they have tons and tons of milk. The bags get sunburned. The mud chaps them. You never seem to gain."

Dodging a kick, she squirted milk into the calf's mouth, stuck her finger in and then substituted a teat. The calf twisted away. "C'mon, I know you haven't sucked this before." Just as the calf began to drink, the mother let go with a tail-end splatter. "Cow!" Susan said, wiping her face on her shirt.

Perhaps this wasn't a good time to talk about fashion.

Susan, twenty-six, is a salaried hand on the Spann

Ranch, a broad-shouldered cattlewoman who feeds bulls and brands. "Susan's our man," her mother had said. But siblings call her the sensitive one, with mothering instincts and patience to solve unending milking problems with newborn calves. "She'll save them when they should have died," said her father.

Behind the blue eyes and manure-splattered face is the mind of a pattern-maker. No one on the ranch knows clothes better. She has a degree in apparel from Colorado State University and a closet full of clothes that she made and rarely wears. Like everyone else here she lives in jeans.

"I always thought that dime-store cowboys bought what looked good," said Susan. "Cattlemen don't care what they wear for image. I dress for comfort, not for style."

Susan studied design as a way to leave the ranch. At the time Ken was the heir apparent, she was the middle of three girls, and "Dad wasn't going to split the ranch up." She designed shirts and outerwear for Miller Stockman, then made patterns for Indian clothing designer Virginia Rumik in Oklahoma. Three years ago, after the ranch was expanded, Susan returned. "It took a long time before a future was offered." Last August, she married Bill Rivale, a muscular cowboy now in college. They have been offered a place in the Spann operation. "It's a lifetime decision to make," she said, "and that's difficult."

She stood back and watched the calf drink. I kidded her about her footwear. "People around here want clothing that's comfortable and serves a purpose, whether it's warmth, safety or protection from the sun and wind. You'll see me in tennis shoes. For me, they're more comfortable, except when I ride."

The Spanns look "western" when they wear hats and pointed boots and kerchiefs on their necks. More often, they surprised me with overalls, tie-dyes—or sneakers. Their guise grew from their experience. They wear chaps when they handle cattle, mudboots when it's wet. They carry a pair of leather gloves and a yellow slicker on the saddle, in case of rain.

Ken has a sweat-stained Resistol hat and wears lace-up boots to support a shattered and pinned ankle. But he also has what he calls his "17th Avenue suit," a Yves St. Laurent from Denver's Cottrells for his lawyer duties in water court.

Ken and Lee own dusters made by Susan, long coats of oiled cloth that have become all the rage in western wear in the last six years. Lee had seen one on TV. I had seen them at the National Western Stock Show in Denver. They look great with boots and a hat, giving already slim cowboys a long, sexy silhouette.

"A duster comes across giving authority," said Susan. "You think of old sheriffs wearing dusters and walking down the street." She made them as a CSU class project to improve on a basic design. Her dusters have knit cuffs, pockets big enough for gloves and big bellows at the back to fit over the cantle of the saddle. Unlike dusters designed for urban cowboys, with a slit in the back that can leak, Susan's dusters keep out rain and keep in the heat of the horse.

Unlike suburban cowboys going to the Stock Show, the Spanns never "dress up." They look natural in western duds—healthy, weathered and trim—but they are not usually conscious of looking the way so many emulate.

One time Ken stepped off a plane at Dulles International in Washington, D.C., with his cowboy hat, cowboy boots and a wool dress coat made by Mary. Not until he caught people staring did he realize how different he looked. When Ken's sister Sandy wore street clothes to a job interview in Gunnison, two miles away, the employer said, "I sort of expected you to come in chaps and spurs."

"People think when you grow up on a ranch, you wear these clothes all the time," said Polly. That struck a sensitive chord in me. I wanted to fit in on the ranch, but the Spanns knew I was no cowboy. I love wearing Levis. But hiking boots with Vibram soles were out. One walk in the barnyard would stay with my shoes for the rest of the day. At Ken's suggestion, I bought a pair of Carhartt bib overalls with a blanket-lined jacket. They are duck brown canvas and much better for pulling calves than pastel Patagonia shells.

My real hang-up was the Stetson—symbol supreme of a cowboy. I felt like a dime-store dude in mine, and probably looked it. The ranch changed all that. I got splattered with blood. The hat rolled in the manure. And I learned the real value of a wide-brimmed hat, the reason the original cowboys, the Mexican *vaqueros*, began wearing them. It keeps the sun off your face.

Lee began wearing a taupe Australian-style brim to cover his face from the high-altitude sun. "I've had four skin cancers removed. One on the left eyelid. That's close enough for me."

That night I boiled some water in the condo and steamed my dirty Stetson into a new shape. Kind of a cross between Indiana Jones and Gabby Hayes.

A meadowlark yodeled to the cowboys the other morning, and I think they could hear it. Their earflaps, for once, were tucked back in their hats.

Like a sunrise, spring has arrived along the Gunnison. Suddenly it is bright and warm. More than half the Spann cows have calved. The night shifts are shorter. Only occasionally do Ken or Susan ride out with flashlights on horseback to attend a cow.

By the time the ranch day begins at 7:30 A.M., the sun is over snowy Fossil Ridge and in the eyes of the four hands who gather around Lee and the Willys for their day's assignments. After feeding hay from dwindling stacks they spread out, burning weeds in irrigation ditches and dragging meadows with rubber tires to break up cowpies before the start of irrigation. The rest of the crew saddles up to ride among the cows and calves. I got to ride along.

"We're looking for something I hope we don't find," said Lee, who strapped white, fringed chaps over his Wranglers. "Getting calves here is the easy part. Keeping them here is the hard part."

He led Skipper from the feed bunk by the red barn and tied him to the hitching post outside the tack room door. He would spend the day horseback doctoring calves for scours, cutting healthy cow-calf pairs into drier sageland and moving near-term cows, so-called "heavies," closer to the calving barn.

It was classic cowboy work, although the Spanns make a distinction between cowboys and ranchers. "All cattlemen are cowboys, in a sense," said Susan. "But not all cowboys are cattlemen."

Lee uses a horse but is not wedded to it. He spends a lot of time on foot, irrigating, haying, doctoring. A cowboy, on the other hand, likes to do his work from the saddle. "I'd rather be doing this than anything else," said Bill Rivale. "I'd rather ride than put up hay, but I'll do it. The one thing I don't like is irrigating. You have to wear those big overboots and have to go on foot everywhere."

The rancher also is tied to the land. Cowboys drift, working a few months here and there for different outfits. The Spanns have hired Mexican labor since 1972—men who leave their families for a summer in Colorado.

Lee entered the red barn by pulling on a leather strap which runs through a hole and lifts a wooden latch inside. The smell of leather and horses rushed out. Eight or ten saddles were mounted on wooden horses, with their soiled blankets on top to air. Wooden barrels—keg sized—filled with horseshoes sat beneath, and loops of bridles hung above. Two-by-four cross pieces overflowed with brushes and combs. In an adjoining room (where the Marlboro cowboys posed in the Dutch door), the Spanns kept the heavy tack for their draft horses: singletrees and collars and coils of heavy leather. Lee handed me a bridle for Jack and pointed to a saddle used by his father. It was an old Porter, made in Arizona with a flat horn preferred by *vaqueros*.

The cowboy owes much of his heritage to the Spaniards who brought horses (*caballos*) and cows (*vacas*) to the New World and who hired lower-class cowmen (*vaqueros*) to herd them through the Southwest. Over the years they adopted equipment still used by Lee today: *los lazos* to lasso calves, *chaparejos* to cover jeans and *espuelas* to spur the horses.

Lee's hired hand, Manuel Castro, is a link to that heritage. He is from Michoacán, Mexico, and comes from a line of *vaqueros*. His father, Ramon, worked on the Spann Ranch in the past, and Manuel brought his brother Miguel to help this year. Manuel, short and muscular with a mustache on his dark face, calls himself a *campesino*, a farmer. But when not growing maize, he rides the *caballo de carrera* as a jockey. A single strap over his knees holds him on.

Manny speaks mostly Spanish, which Ken translates. The rest of the crew communicates with a jumble of English and Spanish: "Manny," Lee will say, "get that *vaca negro*."

We rode into the meadow close to the barn, through dozing calves and grazing cows. Lee weaved around them, flicking them lightly with a buggy whip. The healthy ones reacted with a start. Sick calves are lethargic.

"These cows will tell you what's happening," he said. "You just watch and listen. Cows know when their calves are sick. They'll lick them and try to get them up. There's a cow that won't be around next year. See that cancer eye. ..."

He spotted a newborn, the placenta still over its head, and spurred Skipper to a gallop. Just as he arrived, the membrane fell free. The cow was licking, bawling, urging the calf to stand.

"It's really pretty amazing. They've got to be born, they've got to get up and they've got to suck, and they usually do it in an hour."

It was warm as we rode. Out near the sage-covered foothills that rise behind the ranch, I felt a century away from U.S. 50. Jack cut pairs like a pro. He stayed close to the cow. If the cow changed directions, Jack turned before I could react. We drove them to the corral for transfer to a drier pasture.

"Put you on a good horse and you're not a bad hand," Ken said. He loosed his rope to catch a calf with scours, a type of diarrhea. But Jet, his young black, would not cooperate. Ken threw the lasso three times, but Jet had not yet learned to chase close, and he twisted and jumped as Ken fought for control.

Steve Martin, a hired hand, chased after the calf, swinging his lariat. On the second try, the calf came down. Martin looped the dally around the horn and hopped off. He knelt by the calf and gave it an injection of antibiotics.

"I get to cowboy three months a year," he said. Most of the year he runs a gift shop. "A cowboy doesn't have to be horseback all the time, but when he is, he knows what the hell he's doing."

Ken and Jet were still at odds. Ken yanked the reins. Jet, tired of cows and Ken, took off.

As they rode out of sight at a hard gallop, I could hear Ken saying, "Whoa, whoa."

Some cows are more equal on the Spann Ranch. Martha was one. Sis was another. But the current queen of pampered bovines is Daisy.

While her cow colleagues munch grass and hay, Daisy gets a bucket of rolled oats served in a galvanized bucket. While most of the cattle get dirty, Daisy gets a regular brushing to pull debris and long winter hair from her red and white coat. And while the rest have yellow eartags with a number, Daisy's name is painted on hers.

"When she was a first-calf heifer, I'd bring her grain. She loved grain," said sixteen-year-old Jan Spann. "I leaned on her a lot, and one day I just jumped on her."

Daisy and Jan grew up together on the ranch, from the time Jan was nine and Daisy a one-year-old calf. Today, Jan is a tie-dyed teenager with plans to teach music, and Daisy is her ticket to do it. That one calf has spawned a small herd, enough to put Jan through college. That's how all the Spann children paid for their education—Ken's law school included—with a single heifer at the age of nine, a gift from their father. "I didn't pay for college," said Lee. "I didn't have to."

Daisy had six calves, four of them heifers, and they each had calves. Altogether, Daisy has produced fifteen offspring worth more than $8,000. This one cow, in microcosm, is how the Spann Ranch operates, and how it is able to support three families. Daisy is a basic industry, creating economic wealth from raw materials, sun, water and soil. She turns grass into meat and milk, protein that has value. She also produces, each year, another baby protein machine.

"We're in the business of making meat for people to eat," said Lee. "All that hay we feed in the winter? What we're actually building is that calf."

Wearing her pink Bolle sunglasses and faded jean jacket over a pink cotton T-shirt, Jan demonstrated how she sits on Daisy while Daisy stuck her nose in the oat bucket. "Most people don't realize I live on a ranch," she said. "I've never worn my cowboy boots to school. They've got crap all over them."

Red-haired Jan is Lee's favorite companion on the long summer rides into the high country pastures. He uses her to ride and run a hay rake, work that repays Lee for the year-round maintenance of Jan's herd. "She's absolutely fearless," said Lee. "She's a good hand." So good that some of the "cowboys" at school are intimidated by her. "I can ride better than them," she said. "I'm not afraid of work, either. One of my friends has fingernails that long. She wouldn't do anything to hurt those nails."

The cows raised by the four Spann kids also taught the value of responsibility. The kids kept 4-H records, they showed the animals at fairs. They learned life's lessons of birth and death and hard work. "A ranch is a good place to raise kids. They're needed," said Polly. "There are a whole generation of kids who are not needed, and that's a problem."

When Jan was four, Lee put her at the wheel of the hay truck while he fed the cows. "He'd say turn left, and I'd say, which way is left? We'd hit the ditch and I'd say how do you stop?"

Jan is president of the Country Cousins 4-H Club, enrolled in junior leadership and cake decorating. The club is planning a trip to Denver this summer to take in Elitch's amusement park and the city's museums. There might also be time to shop. A lot of Daisy's wealth, it seems, has gone for clothes. "I love clothes. My sister has a closetful, and I'm always over there." She currently is trying to decide on a dress for the junior prom, coming in a week.

In two years Jan probably will leave the ranch. "Winters are tedious and probably I'd have no future—unless I married a rancher. I want to get out and see if I can make it on my own." If she ends up in music, it will be a gift from her mother. Jan takes private piano and voice lessons from teachers at Western State College. Asked what she got from her father, she said: "These stupid broad shoulders. I have to take the shoulder pads out of everything."

It was high noon on the Spann Ranch, and Leontyne Price was singing in the kitchen. As the calving crew filed in,

Polly Spann stopped the record and began dishing out platters. There was no room for her at the table. She moved behind the chairs, refilling bowls the size of buckets and watching her morning's work disappear in silence.

Someone mentioned how good it tasted, and a murmured echo swept the table. Then the crew filed out, leaving dirty dishes beside the sink. "Hunger makes a good cook," said Polly with a chuckle. She restarted the record and began to sing in Italian, "Un Bel Di" from *Madama Butterfly*.

"I have a hard time defining myself," she said. "I don't like 'housewife.' I'm more than a homemaker. When I fill out forms, I put down I'm a rancher's wife." But that stroke of her pen reveals shortcomings only in language, not in her life. She's too modest to write "rural renaissance woman."

In a patriarchal family where Lee Spann is headmaster, brain and brawn, Polly, his wife, is a remarkable mate, bountiful, strong and soulful. "I like to help wherever. Jan and I irrigate. Lee and I feed. I can lift bales and throw them around. Mary and I spend five days a week on books. Just to say I cook and wash and sew—I don't."

Polly is the pivot between generations on the ranch, a grandmother of two who believes in equal rights. "I'm as liberated as I care to be. I came to this ranch with the man."

But she was also behind the move to change to "Cattlewomen" the name of the "Cowbelles," the women's auxiliary of the Colorado Cattlemen's Association. "When we were first married, Lee took me out to see the cattle. My mother gasped. There are still many ranchers in this community who believe a woman's place is in the home."

Polly's three girls worked with Lee outside and learned to sew and cook inside. "They were honed with an ax," said their mother. "Lee told them: you have to look like a girl, act like a lady, think like a man and work like a horse."

Polly Porter, fifty-five, grew up in Gunnison. Her father, Ralph, was a state legislator and business manager of

Western State College. Her mother, Marjorie, sang beauti-
fully and taught Polly the classics. But she was raised to be a
housewife and quit college after two years to marry Lee in
1953. She was eighteen. "We were a little dubious because
she was a town girl," said Grandma Lois. "She knew nothing
about the ranch. Nothing. But he could have looked the
world over and not found a better one."

Polly looked out the big window facing east toward
Lois's house. Her graying red hair, curled around her
cherubic face, looked almost blonde in the light. A spotting
scope sat on the table. Through calving season she keeps
watch of the cows in trouble, running out to help if no one
else is around. Next to the table sits an easel with a print of
"The Navajo" by Olaf Wieghorst. Behind Lee's chair is a
bronze, "Poco Frio," by Bill Chappell.

"When I look back on it, my Dad was a male chauvin-
ist—'cook and take care of me.' I can't even remember him
asking me what I wanted to be. I tell the girls how lucky they
are to have a father who sits down and talks to them."

On a wall by her sewing room hangs a small plaque
from the Gunnison Bank and Trust Company thanking
Polly for ten years on the board. She left last year, partly
because of the heartbreak of watching neighbors go under,
partly because of a growing cynicism "about people who put
their names on the dotted line without ever intending to
honor it." But the biggest reason was the fear of being sued
for bad loans. "There were times when I thought, I'm
putting my whole family's ranch on the line."

In the basement, Polly keeps an office as the ranch's
secretary-treasurer. Boxes of files and old checks are piled in
a closet. A milk can is filled with maps and architectural
drawings. The "Cattleman's Tax Manual" is on the desk. "I
really do know what's going on around here. And that's to
Lee's credit," she said. "I do defer to Lee. What he says goes.
But I know I have a tremendous amount of influence."

When Lee was in Korea with the army, she returned to school and starred in several musicals, including *The Red Mill.* John Ford, the Hollywood director, was filming winter scenes nearby for *The Searchers* and saw Polly in *The Merry Widow.* "He came to the play and offered me a movie test," said Polly. "I wasn't even interested. All I wanted was for Lee to come home and to get on with our lives. I wanted to live with Lee on this beautiful ranch and ride off in the sunset, I guess."

She giggled at the sound of what she was saying. Today, her lyric soprano is heard around the house, at funerals of friends and in a community choir which practices every Wednesday. Lee doesn't much like her kind of music, but whenever he's out, she slips on a record.

Puccini's *Tosca* is one of her favorites. The opening line to "Vissi d'arte" speaks to Polly Spann. "Love and art," she sings with Leontyne. "These I have lived for."

4

For the Promise of Tomorrow

*T*he horsemen pushed against the snow squall, their hats tipped against the wind. A rim of white formed on the brims as their eyes scanned for signs of a culprit. A ranger in uniform led the group, a posse of sorts, without guns. But the ride was deadly serious; there was a new range war above Gunnison.

"I have hard feelings," said Bill Trampe, a tall, weathered neighbor of the Spanns. "There are too many people in this country." The high country sageland above Trampe's ranch north of Gunnison has a history of conflict. But the new dispute pits ranching against recreation. The U.S. Forest Service, which owns the land, called the ride to try to settle it. Nearly all the players went: outfitters, ranchers, biologists, wildlife experts and bureaucrats—forty-two people on horseback. Ken rode to show support for Trampe. For years their families have shared fencelines and water, they've run cattle together on federal land and they've stood together against encroachments to their livelihood.

For more than a century, livestock have grazed Flattop Mountain; Trampe leases it during the summer. But the government now has designated the area important wildlife habitat. The number of elk has risen, and as a result, the number of hunters and trail riders looking for them has increased.

On the night of December 10, 1988, and continuing every night until March of 1989, hundreds of elk came down off Flattop into Trampe's feed bunks. They trampled fences, they ate tons of hay he had put out for his 700 yearling calves and they charged his pickup when he tried to frighten them off. Even state wildlife workers, who counted 450 elk one night, gave up their attempt to frighten the elk away. As a result, Trampe ran out of hay six weeks early. He figures the elk cost him ten percent of his hay, about $3,600 worth.

He blames pressure from hunters, horse riders, mountain bikers and hikers in the higher country. "There are so many people out there playing that the elk don't like it, and they come down," he told the group, which had stopped on a hillside that swept to the north, toward Ken's ranch and Crested Butte. Vacation homes have spread over traditional elk ground, Ken pointed out, forcing elk to change migration routes. "Their whole flow has been disrupted."

When Trampe complained about the elk in his feed, one outfitter-guide from Gunnison accused Trampe's cattle of overgrazing Flattop, forcing the elk to descend onto his ranch. The outfitter takes trail rides across the land. "People in town said I had no right to bitch because I was on public lands," Trampe told the group.

Under state regulations the number of elk in the Gunnison Valley and throughout Colorado has risen to the highest levels this century, 182,000. The state division of wildlife tries to maximize wildlife according to the land's capacity and then controls the herd size by hunting. But on one section of land adjacent to Flattop, there are 4,000 elk, 1,000 more than the target. Flattop is supposed to carry 200 to 300 in winter, not 600 as it did this year.

"Our charge is to manage wildlife for everyone in Colorado," said Jim Young, area manager for the division of wildlife. "The sportsmen pay the bill. Private landowners winter a large number of native wildlife on their lands and have for years. They create ice cream cones [of hay] that attract wild animals. We aren't trying to favor one specialized group. We're trying to operate to the satisfaction of everyone—and that's not possible, as we found out this winter."

Young believes a severe winter, low hunting success last fall and high birth rates caused the herd to expand. He plans an extra hunt this fall. But ranchers all over Colorado complain that the elk problem has gotten out of hand. One of Lee Spann's neighbors sold his Beaver Creek ranch to the state as an elk refuge after the severe winter of 1983-1984 when 1,100 elk grazed alongside his 550 cattle.

"The animals were really weak and were dying by the hay racks," said Marilyn Elze, whose husband and father operated the ranch. "If we were to starve our cattle every year the way the division of wildlife starves the game, we'd be turned in to the Humane Society. We decided they needed the ranch more than we did."

Lee Spann counted 300 elk outside the kitchen window at times this winter but filed only a $200 claim for damages to hay and pasture. His haystacks were protected by state-built fences.

Trampe refuses to file for damages. He argues that would legitimize elk feeding and not solve the problem. "I'm not in the business of raising wildlife for the state of Colorado."

He also scoffs at suggestions from Young that he could make money from wildlife, perhaps with sleigh riders into the herds. He said he would give the state one more year to solve the problem and then build an elk-proof fence around his property, a move that would only push elk onto neighbors' land.

As the posse rode through well-managed pasture, it was clear that overgrazing wasn't the culprit. Trampe's war is with the changing nature of Gunnison country. Ranching no longer is king. Tourism is the leading industry.

"The National Forests have become playgrounds," said Jim Barry, a range conservationist with the Forest Service. "We can graze cattle, but we have to do it gently to get it done." He said neither Trampe's cattle nor elk overgrazed Flattop. "It's social conflict, rather than grazing problems."

Three times a day, the work stops on the Spann Ranch. Horses are hitched, pickups are left parked by the irrigation ditches and workers file into Lee's basement to doff their coats before eating.

Of all the meals, none is as important or welcome as dinner, the gathering at noon. They call it dinner because it is the biggest meal of the day. While supper is soup or leftovers and "lunch" is a sandwich stuffed in a saddlebag, dinner is the main meal, a time for joking and planning— and answering the phone. Callers know that Lee or Ken, who take no coffee breaks, will be in the house.

More often than not, beef is on the table—cut from their own cows—with fresh rolls, vegetables and salad. Polly usually makes dessert, too, from sorbet to strawberry pie, so fresh it runs at the edges. "When you work outside you realize how nice it is to come in and sit down to a nice dinner," said Polly. She is generous with her food and with invitations to eat. I have sampled steak, hamburgers, stew, chili and spaghetti with meat sauce. Once, we had turkey sandwiches, which I took as an opening to a delicate issue I wanted to raise, one I feared impolitic at a beef producer's table.

"Have you cut back on the beef you eat?" I asked.

"Why?" snapped Lee. His look across the table signaled an answer, not a question.

"Because the rest of the country has," I replied.

"I have low cholesterol," he said, "and I've eaten beef all my life."

I should have expected some resentment from a family whose livelihood is affected by America's eating habits. The Spanns do not believe beef to be problem food.

"Anti-beef—I'm puzzled by it," said Polly. "It's a whipping boy for a sedentary culture."

But the Spanns, nonetheless, have faced the issue thoughtfully and in a businesslike way. In what they raise and in what they eat, they have changed with the times. "For years and years and years our industry was based on fat," said Lee. His father built a herd of Hereford cows, a British breed known for putting on fat, which made its meat tender and juicy. Herefords adapted well to western rangeland, too, and their color made them a favorite subject of western artists. In paintings and photographs collected by Lee the Hereford seems the quintessential cattle breed.

"I'd love to have all red and white baby calves that run and buck and play," said Lee. "I was raised with them." He also was raised before cholesterol was recognized as a health risk. His mother cooked three big meals for the crew on a coal stove. Breakfast included bacon and eggs and hot biscuits with milk gravy and fried potatoes. She would make two big pans of baking powder biscuits, about forty, for each meal. Dinner and supper were variations of the same meal: roast beef and mashed potatoes and brown gravy, hot rolls and a vegetable and a dessert, pie or pudding. She included a salad and lots of white navy beans. "I wanted to be sure they had enough to eat," said Grandma Lois. "I didn't worry about cholesterol."

With the national health mania, however, the Spanns had to reconsider. Three years ago Lee began cross-breeding his Herefords with Salers, a French breed known for leaner beef. "I feel they will be in more demand in the future. Like any industry, if you're going to stay in business, you've got to give people what they want."

At their own tables, the Spanns have reduced fat, which they carefully distinguish from red meat. "Beef is good food," said Mary, a home economist. "[But] I don't think people in the beef industry can ignore the health issues related to beef." She trims fat from steaks, she broils rather than fries. And despite Ken's pleadings, she does not fix fried potatoes or donuts. "Eating as much beef as we do, I keep an eye on it."

Mary chews on each question. Her voice is spare, like her answers. In family gatherings she is the quiet one, often tending to Laura and Andy, her restless children. When Mary was at Colorado State University, cholesterol was not a real issue in nutrition classes. Today, active with the Gunnison Valley Cattlewomen, she faces the problem as she promotes beef. Two years from now she will run the microwave division of the National Beef Cook-off.

Beef, she said, has about the same amount of cholesterol as roast chicken with the skin removed, seventy-five milligrams in three ounces of meat. And only half the fat in beef is saturated, the artery-clogging kind. "People now see they can be healthy and still eat beef. I wouldn't be surprised that Ken has a pretty low cholesterol count, as active as he is."

Mary is tolerant of different nutritional views—if they are based on facts—and resentful only if those views are pushed on her. A gourmet chef visited her home recently, the husband of a college friend. He bragged that he hadn't eaten red meat in three months and had lost thirty pounds. He refused one of Mary's steaks and made his wife drive to town for turkey.

"What else have you stopped eating?" Mary asked him.

"Desserts and fried food," he said.

* * *

Steve Martin waded thigh-high into the sea of calves and shoved a little bull headfirst into the chute. His suspenders bulged as he bent over the balking calf. He pushed with his belly and the calf slipped between the rusted uprights. Ken slammed the chute closed and pulled the top toward him, rocking the whole contraption on its side. The calf was pinned on a waist-high "table," bawling and thrashing, his legs churning. I reached over, grabbed the right rear leg, slipped a noose around it and tied it to a metal post in preparation for branding, castrating, dehorning, vaccinating and implanting. Getting a hand kicked was nothing compared to what the calf would go through in the next two minutes.

For the most part, a calf's life is a picnic. After a nose dive out of its mother, it spends the first six months of its life sleeping, nursing and playing. A calf gains weight at the rate of two pounds a day. In the first month alone it grows from a birth weight of 80 pounds to a branding weight of 125 pounds and develops from a spindle-legged baby to a foot-loose scamp who pays no homage to horses, men or barbed wire.

"See why we don't wait another month?" Ken yelled as I dodged a sharp hoof and wrestled a leg. Ken's head was hidden in smoke, which boiled from the hide where his iron burned. It sizzled and smelled and formed the "T" top of the T-open-A Spann brand. "That's our return address," said Lee, who was bent beneath the leg I held, making the bull a steer. A trickle of blood ran onto the chute, and he turned and tossed the testicles to Rascal, his dog. More smoke rose from the calf's head as Manuel Castro burned a circle where the horns would have grown. The calf, by now, had given in and lay with its tongue out.

What calving is to life on a ranch, branding is to its business. A calf's life course is determined in less than two minutes on the table. He becomes an asset, a part of the corporation. His right hip carries a brand name, as important to the Spanns as McDonald's arches. "When it goes to market, it has our name—our reputation—on it," said Ken. He stuck the iron back in the flame of a propane burner behind him. Its roar matched the volume of bellowing mother cows who stood at the fenceline and called for their babies. They had been separated earlier in the day, driven into the old corral on the edge of the sage hills. The calves waited in a pen, the mothers outside.

Without a brand, the Spanns can't claim a calf as theirs. Under Colorado's tough brand law they can't sell or even ship cattle without a brand. State brand inspectors watch every transaction, and every year they find at least one of the Spanns' animals mixed in with another herd. A check arrives from a sale barn somewhere. The T-open-A is one of 30,605 brands in Colorado. Owners pay the state $65 every five years and thirty cents a head for the enforcement program.

"This is the one time of the year I miss Granddad," Ken said. "He used to sit right there." He pointed to a rusted metal tractor seat mounted on a tire rim where Virgil Spann supervised the spring rite for years. He died before branding in 1983, but his calf table still is used in the same way. The Spanns believe the table is easier on man and animal than the traditional rope-and-drag-to-the-fire routine, still practiced by neighbors.

As Ken spoke, Susan gave the calf two shots of vaccine, for pneumonia and bacteria. Hired hand Dan Zadra punched a tag through an ear. Lee injected a capsule of growth stimulant under the skin of the ear, then bent it double to cut notches—another identifying mark. I untied the leg and Ken lifted the calf upright. The chute opened, the calf found its feet and wobbled off. Before I could turn around, Steve had shoved a heifer through.

Of the Spann's 800 calves, half are girls and half are boys. After spending a summer sucking their mothers on grasslands above the ranch—and growing to 400 pounds—the calves are weaned and shipped to the Spann farm in Delta to spend the winter in a feedlot, eating alfalfa and corn grown there. Over the winter, the calves gain 200 pounds and return for another summer of grazing. These eighteen-month-old yearlings are sold in the fall, at a plump 800 pounds apiece. They spend the last 100 days of their lives in a midwestern feedlot eating corn, converting their "rangy" muscle to tender meat. The 125-pound branded calf is, by then, 1,000 pounds heavier.

Ken burned another "T" on the heifer before us as Lee cut her ear. She did not get a growth stimulant implant because her destiny, more than likely, will be that of a mother cow, not a beef steak.

Implants give the Spann steers a four percent boost in growth, about thirty-two pounds over eighteen months. At current market prices of $1 per pound, that's $32 apiece or nearly $13,000 for the 400 steers in this year's crop. Stimulants have a tainted name in an age of organic eating and Olympic fraud. Europe has banned hormone-treated meat in an action the cattle industry calls a trade barrier. The anabolic compound used by the Spanns, made from corn mold and not a hormone, is banned in Europe but approved and widely used in the United States to increase the conversion of amino acids to protein. It makes more muscle and less fat, said Dennis Lamm, a beef expert at Colorado State University.

Under federal rules, the stimulant cannot be used two months before slaughter. "These rules are for the public safety, and I'm all for it," said Lee. "We eat the meat that we treat. If we didn't think it was safe, we wouldn't be eating it."

Steve shoved one last calf into the chute. The gate closed, I dodged a hoof, and the smoke rose around Ken Spann's hat. A late afternoon wind blew more dust into our ears. Then Manuel turned the propane off. It was quiet for a change. The Spanns had branded 128 calves, which by now were back with their mothers and walking in the sage. In a few days, another herd would face the iron and become part of the Spann Ranch.

The crew rode slowly back to the barn with its white T-open-A above the corral. There hung a sense of passage on the day: a warm weariness from a tough job as old as the West, still done for the promise of tomorrow.

The two young women sat together in a dark alcove of the Cattlemen Inn, outnumbered by empty seats and even by the judges.

"Why do you want to be Miss Cattlemen's Days?" a judge asked.

"It helps bring people to Gunnison and tells people about ranching," said contestant No. 1, an athletic blonde in blue jeans.

"Being a queen is a role model for little kids," said contestant No. 2, who wore a skirt topped by a belt with a big FFA buckle.

The judges looked quietly at the score sheet before them, not quite certain what to ask prospective royalty. No. 1 lived and worked on a ranch. No. 2 didn't but kept a horse west of town, near Lee Spann's ranch. "Used to be, they were all from ranches," said Rick Vader, in charge of the queen contest. "Now, it's getting to be the weekend or city people."

Used to be, too, that nine or ten girls competed for queen of Gunnison's biggest event, a rodeo, 4-H show and parade in July. Thousands of tourists crowd the streets. "There's a big decline in kids our age, as far as kids involved in agriculture," said Heidi Mussman, eighteen, contestant No. 2, who was crowned Sunday after riding her horse for the judges. In her Gunnison senior class of seventy-five, she estimated that only three or four kids live on ranches.

Ranchland still surrounds Gunnison like a mat on a

photograph, setting the tone for the town. But the land supports fewer ranch families—and that is reflected in the number of ranchers involved in Cattlemen's Days, in the mix of retail stores and in policy which, at times, has set Gunnison, population 4,500, at odds with the Spanns.

A few cattle still graze to the edge of Gunnison, to the parking lot of McDonald's. And hayracks still are pulled past the row of motels on wide U.S. 50, but ski racks and mountain-bike racks are more common. At the big intersection, Tomichi and Main, Steve Martin has opened the Golden Aspen, a gift shop. At $4 an hour, he can't make a living as a cowboy.

Tourism today provides half of downtown's income and Western State College 40 percent, said banker Whit Eastman. Ranching provides no more than 10 percent. As a result, Gunnison has developed an odd appreciation for ranching—for the look it gives the countryside. "The thing I think ranching provides is aesthetics," said Dale Howard, Gunnison's city manager. A tourist probably sees it the same way, as a quaint, nostalgic life-style, portrayed by the cowgirl in the parade or the brands burned in the walls of the Cattlemen restaurant. The Spann's T-open-A is above the salad bar. "They think of us like the mountains," said Polly. "We're there, and it's beautiful."

The Spanns spend $250,000 a year in town, for fuel, vehicle repair, wages and insurance. They would spend more if there were still an implement dealer, a veterinary supply store or a better selection of shoes or dresses or irrigating boots. The Spanns also spend several thousand on charities, like the art center. They have led 4-H clubs and given money for plaques. Lee, for a time, chaired the college foundation board. They serve on scholarship committees, the arts council and again this year sent Daisy, Jan's tame cow, to an animal show at the fairgrounds where townspeople got to pet her and her calf.

Last year, Polly and Lee talked to the third grade about ranching. He dressed in his chaps and duster and took a branding iron. "It's really quite amazing," said Lee. "In our own third grade, right here in Gunnison, those kids didn't know the first thing about ranching."

Still, it surprises, hurts and angers him when townspeople act against his well-being. One summer the country club objected when Lee went to turn the water off in a ditch that runs through the golf course. The club wanted to keep its greens green. Lee was ready to cure his hay. After two meetings, Lee prevailed. A city consultant once eyed Lee's lower meadow as a good site for Gunnison's sewer treatment ponds. The Spanns read about it in the paper. The idea was dropped after the family protested.

More recently, the city signed a contract with a water firm that wants to ship Gunnison River water to Arapahoe County. The move would give the city a reservoir but would open a market for water on the ranchland around Gunnison.

"It's not fair for the Spanns, in the business of raising cattle, to impose their needs or desires on a municipality whose business is providing water for humans," said city attorney Russell Duree.

But Lee wails, "Why don't they just leave us alone?" The answer, probably, is the distance Gunnison has moved from ranching. At the animal show this spring, one boy grabbed Daisy's tail and began pumping for milk. Another pointed to her calf and asked what kind of horse it was.

"They are as citified as people in Denver or New York," said Sue Wilson, a member of the Cattlewomen who put on the show. "If you've got a kid coming through here and can't tell a cow from a horse, how can you expect them to understand a rancher's problems? A lot of townspeople take for granted that that green meadow will always be there. It won't be, unless you protect it. And the tourist wouldn't come here if the open meadow weren't there."

5

If the Water's
Not Here ...

S usan Rivale sloshed through a ditch hidden by willows and
began throwing trash onto the bank. Beer cans, leaves, a
plastic milk jug emerged from a pile of goop that was clogging
it. Earlier, she had found a water ski here. Once, in a bigger
canal, a kayak showed up—without a paddler.

"O.K.," she said. "Let's go get the water." She climbed
from the ditch, rolled down her olive-colored hip boots and
climbed into the old Willys. A mile east of the ranch, she
pulled alongside the Gunnison River. A dike of rocks extended into the stream, diverting water into a ditch cut in
the riverbank. One hundred yards down the ditch, the water
washed against a metal dam, a headgate attached to a rusted,
spoked wheel. Susan unlocked a chain around the wheel
and began tugging. Slowly it turned, lifting the headgate.
Water gushed beneath, and a wave washed toward the
ranch. It was time to irrigate.

On the Spann Ranch, May is the month for water and
grass. The runoff from the long, cold Gunnison winter rolls

by the meadows, yellow from stubble dried in the sun. The ditches brim and spill, and overnight the grass turns green. It is the beginning of another cycle on the ranch. With the stacks of last year's grass hay gone, it's time to start again. "You're either raising it, haying it or feeding it," said Lee.

Susan began her daily circle of the ranch on foot. She carried a sharpened shovel over her shoulder with her waders folded down, like a swashbuckler. The 500-acre ranch is cut by a network of ditches, big ones draining to little ones. To spread water on the land, Susan erects a series of dams in each ditch. The bigger dams are wooden gates with removable boards. The smaller sets are nothing but rocks, packed with sod dug by the shovel. The Spanns use old cookie sheets and lids from fifty-gallon barrels, too.

Susan picked up a lid, shoved it across one ditch and banged it with the shovel. The water backed up and spilled from one side, oozing through the grass that sloped away. "I have a seven-day cycle," she said. Each day she moves the water from one dam to the next, so that once a week every section of land—every blade of grass—is washed with water.

The Spanns irrigate 1,400 acres on their three mountain ranches. By August, the grass is taller than ranch hand Miguel Castro, four or five feet. Two tons of hay come off each acre, enough to feed a cow all winter. The key is the water, which years ago turned the sage of the upper Gunnison valley to timothy, brome and clover. The highest ditch walked by Susan cuts a distinct line through the scrubland—sage on one side, hay meadow on the other.

The Spanns pour an enormous amount of water on their land, 500 acre-feet each summer day, enough for a year for 500 lawn-watering Denver families. The difference is that three-quarters of the water on the meadows returns to the rivers. Irrigation raises the water table beneath the grass temporarily. Then it moves on to irrigate a neighbor's field or carry a boater on Blue Mesa reservoir down U.S. 50 from the Spanns.

It is free water, a right under the old decrees passed down from pioneers like Lang Spann, Lee's grandfather, who turned water from the East River onto his ranch in 1899. But it is not water they take for granted—not for a minute. Thirty years ago, Lee remembers, a water commissioner came to the ranch and cranked the wheel of the headgate down, shutting off the water. The Blue Mesa reservoir didn't exist, the runoff was low, and farmers way down in the Uncompahgre valley, with decrees older than Lee's, were "calling" their water from the Gunnison.

"That's how I got educated about water," said Lee. "I'd never been subject to that control. I learned about the water priority system." He learned, as a result, his own rights and vowed to protect them. Today, Lee is Gunnison County's leading spokesman on water, its representative on the Colorado River Water Conservation District. That organization pretty much speaks for the Western Slope on water and has consistently fought the pumping of water to the Front Range.

"Where's Colorado going to play if they take the water down the Platte?" Lee said. "Nobody's going to move to Gunnison if the river is dry."

He pointed to the broiling East River, which runs from the mountains around Crested Butte past Ken's ranch. Earlier in the day, Ken had cranked open a huge headgate on the East River ditch No. 2. Water diverted by another dike gushed through. Yet, in the spring runoff, the river looked untapped as Lee crossed a wooden bridge, herding cows to summer pasture.

The East, the Taylor and the Gunnison they form are among the few rivers in Colorado that have escaped diversion to the Front Range. The Gunnison still is used primarily for agriculture, wetting 264,000 acres. Nearly 1.8 million acre-feet of water pour each year into the Colorado River at Grand Junction.

But now, the city of Aurora and Arapahoe County have filed claims on the Gunnison for what they say is available water. The Aurora project would put a reservoir down the road from Ken's house. Ken filed a court objection to the claims on behalf of the ranch corporation. During calving an Aurora lawyer showed up to ask discovery questions. Ken, up all night with the heifers, sat with the lawyer in his overalls, boots and a two-day growth of whiskers. He was aided by a file compiled by Polly, listing the ranch's dozens of ditch rights.

"My view is there isn't excess water in this drainage," said Lee. While it gushes in the spring, the river runs much lower in July, requiring the Spanns to extend their dike to catch water. "In the average year we put a dam clear across the East River to fill our decree. At Jack's Cabin we take all the water we can get. That's an indicator to me that the upper Gunnison, on a slightly below average year, cannot sustain existing decrees. That's just based on getting out and getting the water."

Moreover, he said, runoff water that appears to be "extra" helps meet Colorado's obligations to California and Arizona, and to endangered fish near the Utah border. The state engineer has said that both the Gunnison and the Colorado have more claims than available water.

It is unlikely, even if Aurora drills a hole in the Continental Divide and begins draining water east, that the Spanns would be hurt significantly. Their water is protected under Colorado law. Aurora would have to pay to deepen wells or dig better dikes. But it would, in Lee's view, open Pandora's box in the Gunnison valley.

The Taylor River, prized as a fishery, would be lowered to a stream flow less than Ken's East River ditches. And a valley so far untouched would become a target of water speculation. Ranchers on the ropes would have a market to sell their water. Just as it happened in South Park and the area around Winter Park, meadows would revert to sagebrush in five years.

"Gunnison has a water-based economy—recreation and agriculture," Lee said. "If the water's not here, we know what's going to happen. If the water is here, we have a chance."

A letter from Denver arrived at the ranch the other day, addressed to "Polly Spann—the rural renaissance woman."

"Judging from the articles in *The Denver Post,*" the writer concluded, "you have made something of your life." Polly chuckled as she showed me the note. That phrase on the envelope, which I had used to describe her, has become somewhat of an inside joke at the ranch. Ken stuck his head in the door one day and yelled, "Is the rural renaissance woman here?" And when Polly ordered supper from Pizza Hut one evening, Lee wondered whether his "renaissance woman" would ever cook again.

"West of the Divide" has been great fun, for me and the Spanns, largely because of the response. Cowboy Steve Martin is now known in Gunnison as "two-loop" because it took him two attempts to rope a calf on the ranch. His cowboy friends read that and rubbed it in. A chemical company offered to send Lee antiseptic packaged in handy plastic dispensers after reading of his struggle with a dying cow. He had washed his hands and sutures in a coffee can.

And Ken hasn't heard the last of his runaway horse. The fact that he rides, brands and tries to rope surprises lawyer colleagues who remember him fresh out of law school as a brash sagebrush rebel in pinstripes. "Does Ken really work?" one of them asked me.

In an interview with a cattle newspaper a week ago, the Spanns admitted that they were highly skeptical of having a reporter tromp through their lives, especially one with a reputation as an "environmentalist." That's a cuss word on the ranch. But they have given me the run of the place, fed me lots of beef—including a half-roasted Rocky Mountain oyster hot off the branding fire—and even thrown a birthday party for me after getting a bank loan to buy all the candles. Forty-five is a lot to blow out.

The ranch series, like the springtime activity, has reached the halfway point. All but fifty of the cows have calved, half of them are branded and work is shifting "up-country," north of Gunnison where Ken and Mary live. The meadows around Lee's ranch, west of Gunnison, are wet with irrigation water now. The cows, calves, yearlings and bulls are being trucked north to fend for themselves on the grassy hillsides around Ken's place. The mountainsides are covered with aspen showing the first light-green blush of spring. The East River is engorged with dirty runoff from the snowfields to the north.

For the most part, hay feeding is over. There still is branding, sorting, doctoring and endless moving of water through the miles of ditches. Manuel Castro, the Mexican ranch hand, is fixing fence nearly full-time. But the twenty-four-hour work schedule of calving has eased. Lee's humor is more evident. One day at 12:30 P.M. I found him napping on the couch. "There goes my image," he grumbled.

Of all the family, Lee was the most doubtful that an outsider could portray his life's work accurately and sympathetically. But he is pleased with the response. Last week, after being named to the state Brand Board and attending his first meeting in Denver, Lee approached a Continental Airlines gate attendant and showed his ticket. "Are you the rancher I've been reading about in the paper?" the attendant said. "I'm from the East, and I've been following the stories."

I expected people west of the Divide to read of their neighbors. Ranchers, particularly, are following the Spanns and are quick to notice little things, such as Steve's "two loops." When a photograph of a Spann Hereford, a beef cow, was misidentified in the paper as a Holstein, a milk cow, fellow ranchers asked Ken, "Milked your cows today?"

But people on the Front Range who don't know the first thing about cattle are following the Spanns, too. I have always felt that Denverites—even those stuck in lounge chairs—love the mountain West. Even the most urban of us are only a generation removed from the land. An uncle or grandfather was a farmer. There is still strong attachment to the Jeffersonian yeoman ideal, freeholder families working the land, from which rose our ethical roots. The Spanns, no doubt, touch nostalgic nerves in people without horses or scenery or land of their own. They do in me. Their work is historic, yet foreign.

But more important to those of us bound by desks and pensions and middle managers: Lee and Ken, Polly and Susan embody a simpler, honest life. Though bound by many forces beyond their control, they, more than most, live by their deeds.

On the flanks of Flattop, a man and his horse inched up a fenceline dwarfed by the mountain. The line engraved dominion in the landscape; its barbed wires cut the country into manageable squares. Manuel Castro walked beside the fence, dressed as usual in an old ski jacket with faded pink stripes down the sleeves. He wore hiking boots, a beat-up hat and a nail apron filled with staples. His bare, brown and scratched hands pulled wire, patched breaks. His only tools were a hammer and pliers. On the horse beside him, in place of a lasso, a large loop of wire hung from the saddle.

For a month each spring Manny fixes fences on the Spann Ranch. There are sixty-five miles of four-strand barbed wire strung on poles of varying condition. Each year miles are damaged by wildlife, cows and snow. "Fences are a constant source of concern," said Lee Spann, Manny's boss.

Invented in 1874, barbed wire broke up the ranges of the West, and fencing law hasn't changed much since. Despite 120 years of settlement, Colorado remains an open-range state. That means the responsibility to keep cattle out of a wheat field, a garden or another ranch lies with the property owner. Along highways, the state erects fences to keep cows out of the road.

The only way for a property owner to collect damages from a cattleman is to show that his cows got through a "lawful fence," defined by statute as three barbed strands on substantial posts twenty feet apart. The Spanns use four strands, on poles sixteen feet apart. On a good day, Manny can make cow-proof two miles of fence, working alone, the way he likes it. "When I'm with others and they do something wrong, it bothers me all day long," he said in Spanish. "When I'm by myself, I know the problem is mine."

Manny, thirty-two, has been a migrant worker since he was nineteen. The first three years he snuck in from Mexico as an illegal alien from Michoacán, the southern province where his family lives. Now he is classed as a temporary resident alien. He has five children, and his wife is pregnant again. He spends one to four months at home and the rest in the United States working. "If I work here, I have a little more money for food for my family, and I feel better about it. When I work in Mexico, I have very little money for my family, to put away for sickness."

Manny has to work for others because of a moral decision made by his grandfather years ago. When the Mexican government broke up private landholdings into communal farms, his grandfather objected. He didn't think it was fair. As a result, he didn't get a share of the commune at his pueblo. Manny reaps that decision. He has no land. If he works for someone else in Mexico he can earn $5 a day.

In the United States he makes six to ten times as much as a ranch hand or citrus worker.

"The first year away from my family it was hard," he said. "I thought about them a lot. It's a long way. But it's necessary." Of the 400 men in his pueblo, 350 work each year in the United States. Manny followed his father to the Spanns and this year brought his younger brother, Miguel.

He knelt by a loose, lower strand of fence. He cut it, wrapped an end around his hammer head and turned the handle like a crank, tightening the wire. He twisted the ends together, banged in a new staple to hold it and moved on. "Quando la vaca push," he said. "Little more, little more," and he giggled. The cows, he said, loosened the wire by reaching through for greener grass on the other side.

"Good fences make good neighbors," said Lee. Where people share a fence, each is responsible for half—usually the right side as they face each other. Where the Spanns face ranchers, there's usually little trouble. But near Crested Butte, the Spanns share a fence with a development called Crested Butte South. "They don't like our cows in their lawns, and I don't like their dogs in my pasture," said Lee.

The Spanns filed a lawsuit over that fence in 1981, after the developer sold lots that extended fifty feet into Lee's pasture and bulldozed his fence down. While the old property line was inside the pasture, the Spanns won the case because they had used the land for thirty-two years. The law of adverse possession requires eighteen years of continuous use. This year, Lee discovered a new telephone company box 100 feet inside the fence, right on the old property line claimed by the subdivision but rejected by the court. "Looks like we're in it again," he said, disgusted.

Across the road, Manny knelt beside another wire. His was not a political job. He just fixed the fences. But someday, he said, he'd like to move his family to this side of the long border that separates the United States and Mexico.

"Always in my mind I'd like to own something for my family," he said. "If the government doesn't close [the border], my family will come. The schools here are better. I'd like to live in the mountains. The mountains are good for me."

It was once an above-average house, with glass in the doors, patterned wallpaper and a separate bedroom for the children. The chinked logs kept out the rain, the layers of paper kept out the wind, which swept down the valley from Alkalai Rim. Early on, someone split Alkalai Creek so that water could run on either side around the house. They'd hacked out ditches and grubbed sagebrush and carved a homestead shaped like a tear. Then they had disappeared.

"A family lived here," said Polly. "You just marvel at what they did with what they had to work with." She stepped through the doorway of the empty house. The roof was mostly sky. The glass was gone. Someone had pasted against the logs layer upon layer of old sheets and newspaper, which waved, tattered, in the wind. Each layer was a year, or was it a family? "A lot of somebody's life is right here," Polly said.

In the saddle formed by Flattop and Red mountains, across the East River from Ken Spann's ranch, the Alkalai water still flows onto the grass. Polly sees to that with her irrigating shovel. But the home and barns and bunkhouse are empty, fallen and sad, a reminder that in ranch country nothing is forever. Who had lived there, and why did they leave? Was there scandal, or did they wear out? What about children? Were there survivors? The ghostly buildings raised only questions and not just idle ones.

The number of ranches around Gunnison has steadily dropped since the 1940s. Land that supported 100 families now carries twenty-seven. Homesteads full of active families just a decade ago have begun a slow slide to abandon. The reasons are many. Old age, illness and death count for some.

The headstones in Gunnison's cemetery, with Herefords and bucking bulls engraved in granite, tell stories. Virgil Spann's stone carries his brand. But the Spanns survived him and prospered. Why?

They worked hard. They made smart business deals. But the reasons cited most by the family have little to do with the skills of cowmen. "I'd basically say health," said Polly. "We're all pretty strong and healthy. We have children interested in the ranch, too." And they've been lucky. "Every time they go out on a horse and have a wreck and walk away—that's luck to me. I've known men I thought indestructible who were killed."

There was luck, too, in the 440-acre Alkalai property, owned by the Spanns since the 1940s. In the late 1970s it stood in the way of a plan by AMAX to open a molybdenum mine at Crested Butte and build a tailings pond below Alkalai Rim. Lee negotiated a trade that swapped that piece for Ken's 600-acre ranch and the farm in Delta. Overnight the ranch doubled in size, allowing Ken and Susan to join the corporation. AMAX then leased grazing rights back to the Spanns. "Once in everybody's life, you ought to be in the right place at the right time," said Lee. "We're the luckiest people in the world today."

But the free-spending AMAX doomed other ranchers in the valley. They borrowed on the inflated value of their land, which went from $500 an acre to $3,000. Some bought investment land on speculation. Some bought new pickups or took vacations. In 1982, AMAX pulled out because of falling molybdenum prices. At the same time, cattle prices dropped, and Texas oil, which had fueled most of the tourism development in Gunnison, plunged. It was a devastating turning point in the Gunnison valley economy.

The Spanns, through the boom, borrowed only to operate and used only cattle as collateral. "Virgil always said, 'If you're in debt sell your cattle, because once your land's gone, it's gone,'" said Polly. Virgil learned his lesson during the Depression when he and Lois borrowed to buy a ranch west of Gunnison. But in 1933 they got three cents a pound for their beef, not enough to pay the animals' freight to Kansas. "We couldn't pay the loan," said Lois. "So Virgil went and told them, you'll have to take the place back. They didn't want it. They canceled the interest that year and lowered it from eight to five percent. After that we did all right."

That lesson is imprinted today in three generations of Spanns. They pay cash for most things. If they borrow, they have the assets—the cows—to pay the debt the day it begins. "If they can't write a check that day, they don't trade," said Si Sievers, a local car salesman who has sold many vehicles to the Spanns. "You don't see them loading up and going to Hawaii." Like most family ranchers, they put their money into capital—cattle, used tractors, the calving barn. Their fences aren't fancy, just functional. A fancy ranch is rarely a working one. "This is the first year in several years that we had any money to spend on tractors or trucks," said Lee. "You can tell when the cattle market is good by looking at our equipment."

Vacations are rare. Lee and Polly took five days and drove to Oklahoma to see their oldest daughter, Sandy, in February. In most years, a visit to the National Western Stock Show is their big break. "People with two salaries have ten times more spending money than we do," said Polly.

She waited out a sudden thunderstorm in the Alkalai homestead. "The work these women did—getting the food, the water. My grandmother was washing clothes when her kids left for school, and still washing when they got home."

Next year Jan graduates from high school, and Polly and Lee will pay the final mortgage on the ranch, which they bought from Virgil in the 1950s. "Then, hopefully," she said, "the next generation will start buying it." Polly stepped outside the old house, leaned on her shovel and looked back.

"This was a pretty nice house in its day. I like to think people who lived here were happy and loved it, and looked out on that beautiful view, and went to a community dance once in a while—besides washing on that washboard and hauling water."

In the shade of the cottonwoods along the Gunnison River, the big bulls lay in wait. They butted heads, they pawed the ground. They got plain ornery when forced to move. "I guess the best way to describe them is horny," said Lee as he fed them.

In a week his fifty bulls would be trucked from the home ranch west of Gunnison to corrals near Crested Butte. In a month they would be turned out with the cows. They would seek out females ready to breed and deliver the genetic future of the Spann herd. Each will father twenty-five calves. "We pick animals for their sexual ability. It's no fantasy thing. It's part of our business." And as plain as the birds and the bees. "It's something you don't talk much about around here," added Polly. "You don't have to."

The Spanns learned the facts of life early. Sexual attraction was as much a part of the gritty world of ranching as birth and death. Their own love lives were played out in the unvarnished cycles of the ranch. The bluntness of life here infused affairs of the heart, too.

When Lee and Polly met as juniors in Gunnison High, he asked her out.

"I said no," said Polly.

"I'll pick you up at seven," Lee responded and she was ready. They went to a show, but before long, Lee was sharing his deepest rural affection.

"He took me out to show me a 'beautiful' cow," said Polly. "Beautiful isn't a word I would have used."

They rode for hours in their courting days, at cow camp and the forests around Crested Butte. "It was heaven. We spent a lot of time together."

For the Spanns' kids, sharing chores with a member of the opposite sex was both a compliment and a courting test. Lee once asked Susan and a date to check the heifers when they returned. Susan checked them alone. The boy didn't want to end the evening in the calving shed.

When Susan was at Colorado State University in Fort Collins, she dated many different men but found bankers and lawyers turned off by country life. "As soon as I said ranch, that would end the conversation. They didn't want anything to do with this side of my life." Bill, Susan's husband, was raised with horses and cattle, and their courtship got off to a fast start in a wet, sloppy pasture. "The first time I saw Bill, he was walking with Susan out in the meadow, irrigating," said Polly. "I said to myself, 'This is serious.'"

Being part of the Spann family means putting up with the rawness of ranch life, the straightforward communication, even the teasing. It's hard to miss life's foibles here. It is no accident that the three oldest children married country people.

After meeting Ken at CSU, Mary was welcomed at the ranch. She tagged after Lee, helping to hold calves during branding, even calves with scours, a nasty diarrhea. "I got it right in the face," she said. "They knew sooner or later I was going to get squirted."

Ken hayed while Mary helped Polly. At night they'd drive to a dance in Crested Butte, with a bottle of champagne hidden in the car. "We were so in love," she said. They broke up a couple of times. She was worried that she would throw her career down the drain. "I don't want to be doing your laundry and cooking your meals," she told him with feminine ire. Today, when she hangs laundry for their two children, he teases her, "Is this the same girl?"

As for Jan, the youngest and the only unmarried child, life may not end on a ranch. She wants to teach music. But she will carry with her all the personality of the place. At her junior prom, Jan nearly ignored her blind date, a boy from Denver.

"We had a personality conflict," she said afterward. "I had a personality. He didn't. I'm very blunt. It runs in the family."

6

Gifts and Grit
Across a Fence

*T*here were more seagulls than cows on Lee Spann's ranch last week. They swooped in flocks over the wet meadows and landed in shallow ponds of irrigation water collected in low spots. Terns with thin legs and long curving beaks tiptoed with them, looking for food.

The cows have gone north, sorted and trucked day after day, to summer range. They are scattered on hillside pastures along the road to Crested Butte. Nearly every day, Lee rides through them. On June 1, the biggest bunch will be pushed onto federal lands where they will graze and grow in the high country.

For Gunnison County stockgrowers, June brings a brief breather between the rigors of spring and summer haying. That's why they hold their annual shindig, a dinner and dance. They let their hair down, belt a few drinks and dance the two-step until the band quits. The stockgrowers association asked me to join them this year. Ken Spann will be the master of ceremonies.

In the years since Lee was president in 1966, the association roll has dropped to ninety-five members from 130. While the number of cattle has remained fairly consistent at about 37,000, the number of ranches is down—a picture reflected statewide. Colorado just isn't the beef giant it once was. More cattle are raised in Florida or California. But cattlemen like the Spanns have retained remarkable standing in their communities. Although they feel their influence has declined, a letter from a stockgrowers association still carries weight with bureaucrats or a legislative body.

"Like the environmentalists, they have power that is disproportionate to their numbers," said David Leinsdorf, one of three Gunnison County commissioners. The county lists 122 ranch families out of a population of 12,000.

When Leinsdorf arrived in Gunnison in 1975, all three commissioners were ranchers. Today only one, Fred Field, is a rancher. But because ranchers own most of the private land subject to county jurisdiction, and control the water, they have much to say. "We get involved," said Ken. "Partly for self-preservation, partly to serve our community—both the town and the industry."

The Spanns speak out at public meetings. Lee is up to his neck in water politics. Ken is a leader on public lands issues and in the local Republican party. They and their neighbors hired an attorney when the county wrote a land-use plan. The plan allows traditional practices such as cattle drives and allows ranchers to build ag buildings without a county permit. The Spanns see such work as guarding what's theirs.

"It gets very basic very quickly when you talk about property rights," said Lee. He talked between bites of a baloney sandwich, sitting in a pickup at cow camp, the Spann's 2,000-acre pasture just south of Crested Butte. We had pulled a mobile home to the camp for the Castro ranch hands, set it on blocks and hooked water and sewer lines.

To the east rose Crested Butte Mountain. To the west, cattle grazed up the face of Whetstone Mountain, an area once considered for another ski hill. All around us were reminders of Lee's power—and his plight.

Vacation homes marched to his fenceline, taxed at $2.50 an acre on one side according to agriculture production and $226 an acre on the other by its resort market value. Lee's 200-acre pasture cost him $500 a year in taxes. Altogether, the ranchland in the county pays less property tax than the Grande Butte Hotel in Crested Butte. "If we were taxed based on the actual sale value, there wouldn't be any ranching business in Gunnison County," said Field. "We'd be taxed out of business."

Between Crested Butte and the ski area sits another piece of property used by Lee and a grazing pool to collect cows for shipping. It is used strictly for agriculture now, but is an ideal site for a commercial development. The town wants to keep it as open space, or place covenants on its use. That denies the Spanns fundamental property rights. Negotiations are underway. "We are fighting constantly," said Lee.

The Spanns' work in Gunnison County is a microcosm of cattlemen politics in Colorado's legislature and Congress—a vigilant defense to prevent inroads into a traditional way of life and business. Many of the livestock laws go back to the 1880s when cattle were king. The Colorado Cattlemen's Association, nine years older than the state, pressed the territorial government for protection of its industry.

One of the first laws compensated ranchers for cows killed by trains. The association's rules on branding, rustling and beef promotion became state functions. As a result, many laws favor cattlemen, and it is nearly impossible to change them. Despite the urbanization of the legislature—today only fifteen of the 100 legislators are considered rural voters by House Speaker Bev Bledsoe—the so-called "cowboy caucus" remains powerful.

Rural counties tend to return their legislators year after year, allowing them to gain seniority and committee chairs, pointed out Dave Rice, a forty-year lobbyist for the cattle industry and the only lobbyist to be honored with a statehouse plaque. "Legislators raised on ranches develop a keen sense of honor, of reality, a good common-sense approach to things," said Stan Sours, a lobbyist for Mountain Bell. "Their philosophy toward government, and life, in general, falls in line with the business community."

House Speaker Bledsoe is a cattleman. The chairmen of the transportation committees are cattlemen. In taxes and highway money, particularly, rural interests are protected in the legislature. Cattle, for example, are not taxed as other business property is. And some rural counties get $22 in state highway aid for every $1 they spend. Urban Boulder County, by contrast, gets just twenty-two cents from the state for each $1 it spends.

In the state legislature, it is also easy to kill a bill damaging to livestock interests. As a joke legislators once presented Bledsoe with a big red stamp reading "Except Agriculture." They claimed he affixed such wording to any law, anyway.

In Congress, too, agriculture still carries a big stick. The 1964 Wilderness Act, for example, allows grazing in any new wilderness area. Attempts to raise grazing fees substantially always fail. Western congressmen listen to their rancher friends. But beyond hardball politics, there remains enormous respect for both ranchers and ranch life.

"There still is a strong rural presence in this state," said Sours. "We still remember when they were our greatest industry. It's an industry the state wants to continue to protect."

* * *

Gifts and Grit Across a Fence

Being a neighbor got Lee Spann into hot water—and cold water—last week.

He pulled two dead and bloated cows from the bracing Gunnison River near Almont so they wouldn't stink up raft rides. He got yelled at by a neighbor who accused Lee of flooding his horse pasture. To appease the man, Ken dug a better drainage ditch. Across the road Lee also herded back behind a fence a bunch of cows that were eating a lawn. The cows weren't even his. He did it out of habit. "What goes around comes around," Lee said in his usual shorthand.

Neighborliness is as much part of the life-style in ranch country as blue jeans. It's a practice that hasn't gone out of style. It can be as simple as giving an unexpected plate of cinnamon rolls. Or as tough as calving for a sick neighbor. Sometimes it's asked for, usually not. In an era of self-interest, it is a refreshing, unspoken gift. "It's just life in a small community," said Polly.

The Spanns' life is filled with acts of neighborliness, given and received. Polly recently fixed a steak dish for a family grieving over a death. She sang at a funeral, too, for an old rancher who died. She remembers when her father was hurt in a car accident, long ago, just as she was beginning to paint the living room. She spent four days in Denver at his bedside and returned to find the house painted, cleaned and everything back in place. Delight Phelps, her neighbor, and two other women had done the work without being asked. "The word gets around in a small community," Polly said. "People show up with their hearts and their food in their hands."

For neighbors of long standing—fifty years in the case of Lawrence and Delight Phelps who live west of Lee and Polly—there is an openness that would astound city dwellers. Machinery is borrowed, and escaped livestock is moved without a word exchanged. When Lawrence was hospitalized one season, Lee herded his cattle from a distant pasture to the corrals. "I didn't ask," said Lee. "I knew they needed to come home."

But being a neighbor also has its rules. The Spanns are friendly but firm. On the first day of hunting season at their new farm in Delta, they kicked sixty-five pheasant hunters off their property. For those who asked first, the ground was open. They used to allow friends to fish the East River that runs beside Ken's ranch. But when one man drove his four-wheel-drive vehicle to the river's edge, digging deep ruts in a pasture, Ken took the keys and kept them until the man filled the ruts.

When someone new moves in along one of their ditches, the Spanns have a little talk with them to explain what's theirs and what's not. The neighbor who yelled at Lee while poking a finger into his chest got an even-toned explanation of Lee's historic ditch rights.

One neighbor, Ernie Nesbit, even has a written agreement with the Spanns. He owns no water of his own but borrows Lee's on weekends to irrigate hay for two horses. In return, he shoes Lee's horses. Last summer, when Ernie was off fighting forest fires near Yellowstone, the Spanns cut and baled his hay. "It was all done when I got back," said Nesbit. "You can't beat those kinds of neighbors."

No one keeps score of such acts. There is no balance sheet. Little acts of kindness just collect like rose petals in a Bible.

When Lee's father died in 1983, the Gunnison Cattlewomen Association brought dinner for the family before the funeral service. There was food for thirty-five people. The funeral was held early in April, at the height of nonstop heifer calving. Ken, just home from law school, was in charge. He called his neighbor, Buddy Phelps, Lawrence's son, also in the midst of calving. "Buddy, I need some help this afternoon," said Ken. "He never flickered. Just as I was leaving for the funeral, Buddy's trailer and horse pulled in, and he got on our cattle."

Near the end of the service, Ken turned around in the pew and saw Buddy tiptoe into the back of the church. He had put a jacket over his blue jeans and come to pay his respects. "I'll never forget that," said Ken. "I'd help them any way I could, for the rest of my life. Those are the kinds of things you remember."

The walls of the Spann ranch house are broken by many frames, filled with landscapes and characters of the West. Some are paintings, held behind glass and hung by wires on hooks in the plaster. But between the paintings are bigger frames, of window glass, through which the Spanns see outdoors. Remarkably, all the scenes resemble each other. For here on the ranch, life is art, and vice versa. "It depicts the way life is for us," said Lee. "If you look out the window, you can see a scene that any artist would paint."

He pointed to a Chuck Wren painting of an Indian riding a horse in snow. "I've been in that same position as that old boy." He dug an arrowhead from a drawer below the painting and tossed it to me. "Those people were here before us." Lee is the family art collector. His house is filled with lithographs and bronzes, photographs and prints— western art both historic and realistic.

"See this one," he said, turning in his chair and spinning a Bill Chappell bronze called "Poco Frio." "All four of the horse's feet are off the ground. Plus, that old boy has a fix on his chaps just the way I have." The bronze shows a horse bucking after being saddled with cold leather. "That black horse that Manny rides will do it all the time. He's cinchy."

Four months ago, when snow was piled three feet deep and Lee was bent against the wind, I asked him if he ever stopped to admire the view. "No," he said. When a photographer followed Lee one morning during calving, he asked Lee if he ever stopped to watch the sunrise. "The sunrise is not on my mind at all," he said.

But in the spring sun, on a horse ride through a meadow of dandelions and wild iris, Lee began to warm up. Out of the wind, eating lunch while stretched out on grass, his horse and dog around him and the whole world stretched out beyond his boots, he sounded more like the art lover he is. "Most of the time we have so many things we have to do, we don't stop and say it's beautiful."

He is more apt to see it in the art he buys, the Remington bronze, the Olaf Wieghorst lithographs. He pages through *Southwest Art* magazine or walks through the Gilcrease Museum in Tulsa, Oklahoma, and sees his life. "I'd buy more if there were room to hang it. If you are around horses and cows, you can immediately tell if it's right or not," said Lee.

"Ranchers like realistic art," said Barbara East, an artist from Collbran who rides herds near the Spanns every summer. "It reminds them of something that happened. They want a story in their art—a pretty picture is out their window." Barbara is famous for two things: for cowboying while riding mules and a very detailed painting technique. She began her career in 1971 by painting western scenes on cigarette papers and selling them in little frames for $3. Today one of her better cigarette watercolors costs $1,500. Mostly she works in egg tempera.

The Spanns own five of Barbara's works: prints of winter feeding scenes and paintings of a corral and a cowboy eating lunch, with his horse and dog beside him. They could all have been drawn at the Spanns'. "When you ride and handle livestock, it's an art," said Barbara, who cowboys in the summer and paints in the winter. "One feeds the other. One keeps the other healthy. I'll never become well known because I don't have the output. But I don't want to get to the point like these ranchers who are not seeing the beauty around them."

Western art is mostly sold to nonranchers, people who probably buy it for the life-style it conveys. Western art is as rich in symbolism as realism. A man on his horse means more than that. But art of the West rarely conveys the drudgery, the misery, the plain hard work of a cowboy or rancher. No one wants to see the West that way, and so the cowboy is forever glorified. Even the Spanns, who have collected a number of Wieghorsts, turned down a dreary, rain-filled picture he painted. One of his cold winter scenes hangs in the bathroom. And photographs of their ranch show not hardship but cattle in flowers in beautiful mountains.

I could understand a city dweller buying western scenes to hang on his wall. But why a rancher, who sees them every day through a different frame?

"Maybe that's indicative that I'm satisfied with who I am and what I do," said Lee. "I don't have to satisfy myself by looking on my wall for something different."

7

Moving to Higher Ground

*A*ndy Spann couldn't begin to get on the horse himself, but he was dressed for the occasion. He had his cowboy boots, his cowboy chaps, even his cowboy belt around his jeans. His black hat nearly came over his ears. Mary, his mother, lifted him on Skipper, then he shooed Mary away. Sometimes a two-year-old just has to take the reins himself.

For Andy and his four-year-old sister, Laura, each day brings a gradual emersion into ranch life. They rise each morning to ride in the pickup while Dad drops hay for the yearlings. They call the steers "big kids" and the calves the "babies." Driving to town, they ask whose cattle are in the pastures they pass. They love to wear western duds. As they age, Andy and Laura will grow into the ranch, doing chores, riding the range, defending their future from outsiders.

There is an assumption on the ranch that there will be a tomorrow for them. Nearly everything the Spanns do is for tomorrow. They see life as a circle, going 'round and 'round. And that makes them pretty good environmentalists. I mentioned that to Ken one afternoon while we walked the meadows behind his ranch, irrigating. We slopped along in hip boots, a shovel on his shoulder, a pitchfork on mine.

"You calve and brand for a future sale, you irrigate in spring for summer grass, you hay in August for winter feed," I said. "And you doctor, cowboy and generally fuss with your cows so that next year, you can do it all again."

Ken lifted a dam to release the water. It rushed down the ditch to flood another section of grass. I pitched driftwood and trash onto the banks.

"I never thought of it that way," he said. "But the steers are for October, this grass is for September. This ranch is for Andy or Laura."

"An environmentalist works for tomorrow, too," I said.

He thought about that awhile, not quite willing to share a bed with an enemy. "Some people whose views are very close to ours are called environmentalists," he said finally. "Some people who are very radical, like tree-spikers, are also environmentalists."

He walked the ditch, cutting notches in its rim so that water could seep out. "The first year we had this ranch, we got 240 bales off this fifty-acre piece. Last year we got 3,200."

Ken's ranch was the original family homestead, but an aunt sold it. In 1981, the Spanns got it back in a land trade. It had been abused. The meadows had been overgrazed, which reduced the amount of grass plants per acre. In addition, hay had been cut for feeding elsewhere, and the irrigation system had been channeled into a few big ditches.

The Spanns dug smaller ditches to distribute water everywhere. They fed hay to their cattle during the winter on the meadows, which released seeds and manure. The only year they spread commercial fertilizer, the grass grew so thick they couldn't cut it. No other chemicals were used.

"See how close that grass is here? See how close the plants are? We changed that by managing the ground better." The ranch's hay production rose from 8,400 bales in 1981 to 21,000 last year.

"I think you're an environmentalist," I said.

It was half a joke, based on a continuing discussion with the Spanns, who regard environmentalists as threats to their livelihood. They lump into the environmental pot all manner of outside forces: mountain bikers who leave gates open, Crested Butte planners who would control use of ranchland around the city, Earth First! terrorists who blew up a California livestock auction barn and national groups opposed to grazing on public lands.

"I think there are really good things that these interests have done," said Ken. "They have raised us to a higher level of consciousness about environmental matters." But they do not, by and large, make their living from the land. And that, he said, is the real issue.

When I asked Ken's dad, Lee, how an environmentalist would run the ranch, he answered, "That would depend if it were an environmentalist with a trust back East or an environmentalist who has to make the ranch pay."

In two months together on the ranch, the Spanns have impressed me with their conservationist attitude. They do some things I wouldn't: they shoot coyotes, they spray the insecticide 2,4-D on sage, they implant hormones in steers. But they also move cattle if pasture grass gets short. They practice husbandry, the art of making a sustainable living on a piece of ground. They think about the consequences of today's action on tomorrow, because they plan for Andy and Laura to be around.

"We are in this business to extract a living from the ranch," said Ken. "Dad always said don't graze the ground too hard, because we're going to come back next year. And the only ones we hurt are ourselves and our livestock." He turned to me with his shovel on his shoulder. "You've nearly got me convinced. Maybe I am an environmentalist. We have to do it environmentally sound or it won't work."

As the calf spurted away, I turned Cookie's head and jabbed at her ribs with my heels. I braced for a gallop. I planned to cut the calf off, to move him back to the herd. As we pitched down a hill, Cookie's head went down, and I began to fall out of my saddle. The rhythm I expected never came. Instead Cookie crow-hopped and nearly threw me off. I hauled on the horn and pulled myself upright. Manny and Bill got the calf. They could see a bucking bronc had nearly put me in the sagebrush.

"I heard you had a wreck," grinned Lee when we all returned to the cluster of cows and calves on the hillside. "When that head disappears, you know you're in a lot of trouble."

I was embarrassed, but Cookie had put me through another small rite of passage. The Spanns have done pretty well in protecting me from the dangers of ranching. I jammed my thumb branding, I got slivers galore and I nearly got my head knocked off when a 1,000-pound cow charged through a chute, slamming the gate open. I ducked just as a bar on the gate hit my hat. "That was a 1,000-pound bar," said Lee with a whistle. But it was peanuts compared to what the Spanns have gone through.

Wrecks are a way of life on the ranch. Daily work with big animals and rough tools ranks cowboying third in dangerous professions. Only steelworking and logging are worse. A horse weighs more than 1,000 pounds, a bull can reach 1,800. They are worked in difficult terrain in all kinds of weather. "There's a lot of speed and a lot of power there," said Lee. "You can get in trouble so quick."

The Spanns limp, they grimace, sometimes they laugh at the memory of an accident. They run their hands over their athletic bodies and stop at scars or healed breaks in the bones beneath. "It's just normal," said Lee. He pulled off a sock to show toes mangled by too many cows walking on them. "It happens to everybody who's in this business."

Lee can't count the number of times he's been bucked off a horse, and he can't remember his worst wreck, when a dog spooked his horse and it rolled on him.

"I can remember seeing those four feet in the air," said Polly, who hurried to Lee. They were way out on Red Mountain, on summer range.

"I'm fine," he said to her when he got up. "Don't let those cattle get away." But when she returned, he was sitting on a rock, holding his head and asking, "What are we doing up here?" She rode him down and put him to bed. The next day he couldn't count bulls in a pen. He had memory lapses for a week.

Every member of the family has been hurt. Jan was bucked off when her horse walked into a hornet's nest. Mary was ripped from her saddle by a tree. Bill, who rides broncs in rodeos, has had more accidents on the ranch than in the ring. "The worst wreck is a hangup, where a foot gets caught in a stirrup or some other part of the saddle," said Bill. The rodeo rule is to turn on your stomach if being dragged by a horse. The toe then slips out. "I like to eject," he said.

For sheer wreck numbers, though, Ken wins. When he was nine, he crushed his foot on a tractor drawbar while riding with his mother. He broke his arm when his father tossed him across a deep irrigating ditch. When he was a senior in high school, a horse slipped on an icy road and landed on his foot, breaking five bones.

Two years ago that same foot was crushed in a car accident while Manny was driving to town for groceries. The little pickup skidded on ice and turned broadside into a car. Ken's lumbar disc was compressed and a bone in his ankle shattered. While recuperating, he received calls from three neighbors, Buddy Phelps, Bill Trampe and Ernie Nesbit. They all recommended that he wear a lace-up boot to give better support. Buddy and Bill had crushed feet, too.

Last winter, while chasing elk in the snow, the normally reliable horse, Jack, fell and pinned Ken's leg beneath him. They were lying head-down on a steep hill and the horse couldn't get up. Ken calmed him, then looped the lasso around Jack's hind feet. He pulled the feet up and over, rolling the horse over him in the snow. With his feet now downhill, Jack could get up.

Ken wasn't hurt in that one, but he limps often from his previous accidents. He walks with his feet turned out, and his back hurts when he's tired. Fortunately, the bruise on his nose is gone. Mary gave him that shortly after they were married, when they were chasing a runaway bull at cow camp. She was wearing new sneakers and had picked up a two-by-four to protect herself. When she came to a dirty ditch, she decided to throw the board at the bull rather than jump and get her sneakers wet.

She hauled back to throw just as Ken leaped the ditch. The board caught him between the eyes. He sank to his knees beside the ditch. Mary bent to him. "Don't touch me," he said.

Later, Polly tried to ease Mary's conscience. "I've been married thirty years," she said, "and I haven't had the chance to get a lick like that."

The big cubes of salt made ungainly lumps in the canvas bags slung on the packhorse, Peaches. She carried five cubes weighing 250 pounds, and she panted when we climbed a hill. "You sure can hurt a horse this time of year," said Lee, pulling Peaches behind him.

He set out across a meadow from the abandoned homestead on Alkalai Creek. The horses walked through grazing cows and frisky calves which bucked and ran aside.

Through a barbed-wire gate, Lee spurred his horse up a path worn in the sagebrush. It meandered across and up Red Mountain. We were now on U.S. Forest Service land.

Lee stopped and fished a salt cube from the pack, dropping it on a trampled spot. The cattle to follow would sculpt the blocks with rough tongues. Then they would graze nearby. "We'll be on here two weeks," said Lee. "Then we'll move off to allow for fresh feed and new growth for next year." He mounted and headed higher, to drop more blocks on the range.

In June, half the Spann cattle take to the high country, nearly 12,000 acres of federal land between Gunnison and Crested Butte. It is country that dwarfs a man and the 1,200 cows, calves and yearlings allowed the Spanns. The mountains climb in gigantic bounds, broken by streams, clumps of aspen and rock outcrops. This is foraging land— not good, Lee will tell you, for anything else.

The 568 cows graze grass, drink water and lick salt, growing fat. The calves suck their milk, gaining 300 pounds over the summer. The 86 yearlings will gain 250 pounds apiece. By October the yield from this rough country will be 95 tons of beef for the Spann Ranch.

Grazing public lands is a heated issue in the West, where increasing numbers of recreators object to cowpies, and environmentalists decry overgrazing and cheap fees. "People have discovered the West," said Lee. "They discover that people have been using it for a long time, and they wonder why."

The answer is both economic and historical. In the mountains, the best land was homesteaded, leaving 80 percent of Gunnison County in federal preserves. Grazing was an early use of federal land, even before the Gunnison National Forest was created in 1906. Nearly three-fourths of the forest is grazed today.

Summer grazing allows ranchers in the valleys to raise hay on their irrigated meadows for feed through the long winter. The Spanns have followed that routine at least since 1927, when Lee's dad, Virgil, won a permit. Then, as now, a federal grazing permit was a bargain. At $1.86 a month to graze a cow and calf, the Spanns will pay $4,544 for their cattle on public lands this summer.

Lee argues that grazing is an appropriate use of U.S. forests, helping to maintain a community of ranchers. And expenses beyond the federal fee make costs almost as high as leased private pasture. Labor costs the Spanns $40,000 on federal permits. Lee says his family works its tail off to maintain the land in good condition. "We use a piece of ground, then we move off it and let it heal," he said.

Salt is one tool to move cattle. So are horse rides, twice a week, to scatter cattle that congregate around water holes and streams. Lee and Jan ride together much of the summer, watching for sick cattle as they move them.

Near the top of a ridge, Lee stopped in an aspen grove where elk had ripped a fence down. He got off and began stretching wire. The Spanns erect and repair fence to break up the range. The U.S. Forest Service pays for material, the Spanns do the work. "Is it a subsidy?" asked Lee. "If you were here all summer, perhaps you'd think differently."

But the charge that rankles Lee most is misuse of the range. There is every evidence that grazing done well improves grassland by stimulating deep-rooted perennial plants that hold the soil. The rule of thumb is that cows eat half the forage and leave half. "See this litter on the ground?" he said. "That's the stuff that wasn't eaten."

Test plots on the Gunnison forest show that grazed land does as well as, or better than, adjacent land left alone. The Spanns' lease is considered in fair to good condition and improving, according to range conservationist Jim Barry. Because of that, Lee has pushed Barry to allow more cattle on his permit. He asked for twelve more cows near Alkalai Creek and was denied in a nasty proceeding that left bad blood between the feds and the family. Barry even cited Lee for trespassing cows beyond his permit date.

"I feel we have taken good care of the range and that it will carry more cattle," said Lee. At one time Red Mountain and adjacent Flattop carried 2,000 cattle, too much for the range. The Forest Service cut the number in half in the 1940s. "From the time we took the 50 percent cut, we have not received back one cow, with all the spraying we've done and water developing and fencing," said Lee.

"We don't come out and hammer this. We want to turn out again next year. But an increase would allow me to get some return on my investment. We built two-and-a-half miles of fence on this allotment to manage cattle, and we're getting nothing for it."

Without the federal grazing permit, Lee estimates he could run half as many cows. Winter is so severe and expensive in Gunnison that the public lands balance the costs, he said.

The U.S. Forest Service is committed to multiple use, including grazing, but public pressure can change that. Half of Lee's lease area now is considered primary big-game habitat, and he is unlikely to win a cow increase there. The town of Crested Butte also has offered to pay the Forest Service the equivalent of a grazing fee to keep cattle off land above the city. And such groups as Earth First! have pledged "cow free" western land.

"They won't kick us off," said Lee. "They're going to make it so tough that we'll leave."

"C'mon," Ken yelled across the meadow of cows. "To the mountain!" He slapped his rope against his saddle. He spurred Jet forward into the herd. The distinctive bawl of moving cattle rose along Alkalai Creek.

"C'mon," he yelled. "Let's go. Move it." Nearly 400 mama cows and their calves headed up Red Mountain. For the Spanns, the spring routine was over; turning cows onto pasture is an act of summer.

It had been three months since I'd heard the bawl of a cattle drive. On a day that snow pelted our backs, we drove the pregnant cows down the road, away from this mountain valley to the calving grounds at the home ranch. Now we were back: Lee in his pale chaps and Jan in her Dallas Cowboys T-shirt rode the sage bench above the willows. Manny moved into the shaded creek bottom. Bill took the high ground to the north. Ken and I swept the fenceline. The cows began to stream up the mountainside.

In a few days I would be gone, but the life of the ranch would go on: long rides through the cattle, cowboy doctoring for foul foot, pinkeye and bloat. The bulls would be here in two weeks, breeding the cows still nursing their calves. Haying would last until mid-September when the yearlings are sold—payday for all this work. The new calves would be weaned at Thanksgiving, and around Christmas Ken would once again haul out the team and the sled and begin six months of feeding in waist-high snow. That's where I began with this family.

As we climbed the hill, a few calves split and ran. Manny chased one at full gallop and roped its head. Bill cut off a pack heading to the stream and pushed them back into the herd. Three months ago I might have thought it romantic, chasing after calves. Not now. I had come to see life on a ranch for what it is: hard work, a business, a point of view. I had gained the perspective of walking in different shoes: boots, waders and insulated pacs. From horseback, the view is different.

I kicked Cookie across an irrigation ditch lined with delicate blue flag iris. I used to think they were pretty. Now I also saw them choking the meadow that Polly irrigated. We

climbed into the sage sprinkled with phlox, Indian paint-
brush, coral-colored honeysuckle and blue larkspur. They
were beautiful, but larkspur is poison to cattle.

Castle Peak rose in the distance. A little higher we
could see the Maroon Bells. "I see these mountains different
than somebody in Aspen," Lee said. I knew what he meant.
Never again would I see pastoral Colorado the same way.

A wind came up and we slipped on jackets and rode
for a while to the sounds of the ranch: the squeak of leather,
the grunt of our horses, the cows and their calves calling
each other. Before nightfall they had to pair up or they'd
return to where they'd been, along the creek. Their bawls
bounced off the aspen leaves on the hillside above us, an
echo of a phantom herd. Those trees had seen a lot of Spann
cattle pass by.

Down in the valley, I could see the pasture where Ken
first took me for a ride on the haysled. It was ripe and green
now, brimming with water across a field where the Spann
operation began ninety years ago. We had caught those
scenes in pictures and words over the last few months. But
the worst thing I could do was freeze the Spanns into some
nostalgic Americana picture. To survive they had to change.

"For a lot of years I've walked behind the team to
keep warm," said Lee. "It's not a romantic thing to me. It's
too tough here in the winter when it's two hours to a decent
climate."

The Spanns are eyeing another farm in Delta where
they can raise more hay on 160 acres than Susan can on 500,
irrigating every day. They could keep their cattle there in
winter at less cost. And calving could begin earlier, out of the
brutal spring storms of the high country. Susan and Bill
could then have a place of their own.

Movement to warmer climate had been continuous
in the Spann family. Lee's grandfather, Lang, first homesteaded near Crested Butte Mountain, but deep snow forced

him to Jack's Cabin, halfway to Gunnison. Virgil and Lois had lived there, but moved even lower to the home ranch west of Gunnison. "I'd like to break that chain of raising it, haying it and feeding it, if I could," said Lee. "Ultimately we won't feed in winter here. I may not be around, but ultimately that will happen."

The Spanns will remain commercial beef producers, churning out calves for tomorrow's beef market. But the cattle will spend only their summers in Gunnison, grazing the good grass that lines the valley floors and climbs the mountains on either side. Only nostalgia would mourn the passing of a team churning through snow. It is a beautiful picture. But so is a family on horseback in summer, pushing cows and calves to the high country. It is country big enough to break a family—or make one.

As we rode across the breast of Red Mountain, I pulled up in the sunshine to watch the Spanns working their cattle. They didn't notice me. They were moving to higher ground.

The Knights

of Ute Mountain

8

Typical in the Old Way

*T*he lightning arced across Ute Mountain and caught the dancers in the dark. It froze them as a strobe would, in painted moments of ancient ones. Then it rained. In the glow of a campfire their bodies glistened yellow and red. But they kept moving in their sun dance quest, no doubt aware of a greater power.

"We always get rain," said Terry Knight, the sun dance chief. "It's a sign, a blessing."

For more than 100 years the Ute Mountain Utes have held their dance, seeking such signs from their god. They fast, they dance, they meditate in a search for power, for themselves and their people. "You dance to show the Creator you are alive and well and making tracks," Terry said. "Good tracks on mother earth."

The Sun Dance is held each July in a high mountain meadow dotted with evergreens. The mountain is both sentinel and namesake for the reservation and its people. The Ute word for the peak means "mountain with yucca."

White men call it the Sleeping Ute. It is the last spur of the Rockies in Colorado's southwestern corner. The reservation that surrounds it is the last vestige of what once was the Ute mountain kingdom.

The Sun Dance is held near the big Ute's heart, facing east to catch the sunrise. "East is the direction of life," said Terry. "We believe we came from the sun." He stood at the back of a high, round corral made of logs and cottonwood branches, open to the east. On either side of him were fifteen men, young dancers in the midst of a fast. They were bare-chested except for ochre painted on. They wore long skirts of beautiful colors. They held eagle plumes in their hands.

Before them, in the center of the corral, stood the sun dance pole, a cut cottonwood shaped like a huge upright slingshot with willows laid across the crotch. The pole, said Terry, represented the entity, the channel to the Creator.

Night and day, for four days, the dancers charged the pole and retreated, back and forth in a personal gait. There were shuffles, hops, a prancing kick. While they blew whistles made from eagle bones, their bare feet marked a twenty-five-foot path in the dirt. "Making tracks with your feet, making tracks with thoughts and sacrificial manner," said Terry. "You're presenting yourself to the Creator by dancing to and from the sacred tree."

It was mesmerizing to watch. The word primitive came to mind. But that carried an erroneous sense of backwardness. This was no folk dance or costumed recreation of an old art form, a pictograph sprung to life. The dance was beautiful and complex, transcendent of one-dimensional stereotypes so often made of Native Americans: the warrior war-whooping, a weaver on her knees, a chief in his bonnet saying "How." The Sun Dance is living history, a living faith, one tied to the very identity of those dancing and watching. To dance is to *be* Indian.

I went to the Ute Mountain Ute Reservation to write about Indians in more than one dimension. I knew that contemporary Indians did not match my early images. The first Indian word I knew was Seneca, the Iroquois name of a lake I could see from our house in upstate New York. The nearby village was Catharine, named for the Indian queen who ruled the clan by the lake. But they were long gone, pushed out in a scorched-earth policy by General George Washington.

So, the first Indian I heard was Tonto, on the radio. His simple dialogue colored my perception. And my first Indian lesson came from Straight Arrow, a fictitious character used by Nabisco to teach "Injun-uity" campcraft. Instructions for lean-tos and fire spits were printed on the cardboard separators in Shredded Wheat.

In the 1970s, when I moved west, I carried all that stuff in my head. It was 100 years after Custer's defeat, and a new sensitivity was sweeping the country. The tribes then were fighting in the courts for water, coal and land rights. *Bury My Heart at Wounded Knee* had just been published, and I traveled to Pine Ridge to see the grave.

In time, the cardboard cutouts of my youth filled with the blood and flesh of real Indian people. I saw their personalities, humor, dreams and disillusion, their welfare and will. In short, their common lives. I wanted readers to see them too. I wanted them to know people like the Knights.

Terry and his family have deep roots and abiding love for the Ute Mountain Ute Reservation. They are, as Terry put it, "typical in the old way." They have seen a bit of the world but choose reservation life.

Their patriarch is Charles Knight, eighty, a livestock producer and an elder in every sense of the word. His hard work—and spirituality—passed to his children. His ex-wife, Kate, who is also eighty, brought discipline to the household. Her children still call her "the General." She's the one who insisted they go to school every day.

Charles and Kate have six children:

Terry, forty, a college-educated, former Air Force F-4 crew chief, recognized by many on the reservation as a spiritual leader, a medicine man. He wears his hair long in back. His face, like his father's, is long and stern—until he smiles. He can look through you with the steadiness of an owl.

Judy, forty-six, vice-chairman of the tribe, who negotiates tribal water and energy deals. Her face is chiseled and dark; she is often angry, nagged by tribal troubles.

Carl, forty-eight, who runs five ranches with hundreds of cattle owned by tribal members. He's the cowboy, handsome and hefty, but he hides behind aviator glasses.

Gladys Knight Hammond, fifty-three, an administrator with Indian Health Services, which runs a medical clinic at Towaoc (pronounced TOY-yahk), the headquarters village that sits below the sun dance site. She is good-natured, a forgiving mother whose house rings of extended family.

Two other sisters, Elsie and Catherine, live off the reservation.

The Knights live where they always have, on a dry 595,000-acre reserve. It is Four-Corners country, flat and forever, broken only by mesas on the east and dry washes. The Mancos River bed cuts through but rarely runs with water. Except for 325 people who live in White Mesa, Utah, northwest of Ute Mountain, nearly all the 1,675 tribal members live in Towaoc.

Charles was born fourteen years after the reservation was settled in 1895. "That time no highway," he said. "We just ride on our horse. We didn't have good shoes or coat or hat. We just have a blanket." He crossed his thin arms with the memory. For years Charles rode fences between the Navajo and Ute lands to keep Ute livestock in. His family lived in tents, hogans and a stone house away from civilization.

"I did not live in a house when I was young," said Judy. "Bob says I've become civilized." Her face cracked into a giggle. Judy has been a tribal council member for ten years, and she spends much of her time explaining to tribal members the intricacies of budgets. "It gets very interesting, especially when you have to explain accounting in Ute."

The older Knight children were raised in large part by their grandmother, a typical arrangement among Utes, whose sense of "family" is both extended and relaxed. Judy, for example, raised two children plus two nephews and a niece after a sister died. She now is raising her grandchild. "We're all brothers" is a typical explanation.

At the sun dance site, many of the Knights set up camp beneath shade trees away from the ceremonial arbor. Terry erected a teepee. Kids wrestled with wall tents. Judy and her husband, Bob Frank, parked their big RV nearby, set up chairs, a wooden pantry and a card table with pots and pans. They tied a chow named Griz to a tree and tried to keep an eye on Gerrael, Judy's three-year-old grandson.

The family was there to support Terry, but the ceremony was as much for them—families, tribal members, the congregation—as it was for the dancers. "It's like when I go to church. I get the same feeling," said Judy, who brought fresh willow sprigs from a nearby spring to hand to the dancers during a break. The dancers, who ate or drank nothing, touched the cool greens to their bodies. Then Judy joined her sisters near the drum to wave willow branches and sing.

While Terry danced, brother Carl drummed and piled wood for the fire. Carl helped build the dance corral, and like all the Knights speaks easily of spiritual matters. They were raised outdoors, hauled in wagons and made part of ceremonies like the Sun Dance from an early age. "I never let go of things I grew up with," said Carl. "When I drive along and see a flower, I ask where did it come from? Who put it there? There's a long story to that."

As the sun dance day turned to night, and day again, the crowd at the corral grew. They lined up around the circle and crowded the opening to the east. Judy carried more willows. Her son was dancing, too. Charles walked slowly to the pole and spoke to the dancers in Ute, urging them on.

From his side of the pole Terry stood with an eagle wing and prayed for people who came forward. A man in a wheelchair, a child. His own mother, Kate, a small, frail woman suffering from a gall bladder ailment. Terry dusted her with dirt and fanned the wing over her. "I admitted doses of good blessings," he said later. "From grandfather the Creator, the four directions, and dust from mother earth, the substance we are created of."

The Sun Dance ended with a special ceremony in which the exhausted, dehydrated dancers drank a clay-and-water mixture. Outside the arbor, gifts of cash and linens were given to visitors by the sun dancers' families. Then they held a feast.

Books have been written about the Indian Sun Dance, the tenor being that it brings power to the disenfranchised and redemption to the troubled. I asked Terry about the benefits.

"Weight loss," he said with a quick grin. Then he answered: "Spiritual rejuvenation, self-satisfaction. A general overall good feeling. As soon as it's over, you're looking forward to next year."

When I saw the Knights again, the cottonwood leaves on the sun dance arbor had dried and the scrub oaks on Ute Mountain were beginning to turn their autumn hues. It was time for another dance, the social Bear Dance, probably the oldest in the tribe's repertoire. The Utes of Towaoc hold one in June. The small settlement of White Mesa, which hugs a high, windblown corner of Utah, holds another over Labor Day.

When I arrived, a huge circle, perhaps 200 feet across, had been constructed with cedar. It was open to the east, too. Several concession stands were selling mutton stew and frybread. Many people were gambling with cards and the hand game, an Indian version of "button, button, who's got the button." On blankets circled with Navajos and Utes, bets flew fast and furious, up to $100 per hand.

"We're looking for the $2 table," joked Bob. An easygoing, ex-chairman of the Washo, Nevada, tribe, Bob is an anchor for Judy in her public life. He sat behind her as she played the hand game. While three teammates sang and beat a small drum, Judy switched two plastic "bones" in her hand—one striped with paint, one unpainted. The other team guessed which hand held the plain one. Judy's team lost but the double elimination competition went on into the night under lights set up in the cottonwood.

Judy began to dance while Bob went off to watch a mud bog contest where big-wheeled pickups ground through a trough of mud. "Another traditional Indian pastime," said Bob.

According to Ute legend, the Bear Dance began long ago when a female bear taught a young Ute man to dance in a dream. Her movements, her shuffle, when she emerged from her den, became the steps of the springtime rite. After the long Colorado winter, Ute families used to gather for the bear's dance before heading into the mountains to hunt and gather.

The females choose dance partners by walking around the perimeter of the circle that is lined with boys and men and flicking their shawls at one. The women then line up, hand-in-hand, facing the men, who hold hands, too. The lines sway back and forth, two steps one way and three small ones back, to the beat of the bear's "growl." Years ago, a notched stick held against a hollow log was rubbed by another stick to make the growl. Today they use a notched ax handle on corrugated tin. Amplified through a microphone the growl is infectious, insistent.

The dance began in the afternoon and lasted until the setting sun slanted across the mesa, casting a long shadow in the sand of the arena. Exaggerated images of cowboy hats, shawls, braids and feathers stretched behind the dancers.

Charles Knight danced as he had for much of the century. He was dressed in his best—a flowered shirt, a buckskin vest with a beaded rose and an eagle on the back. His leather gloves were brightly beaded.

Judy, near the end of the line, moved her feet in beaded buckskin. The autumn sun bathed her face, the yellow fringe on her shawl, her yellow dress with the beaded belt and a yellow button at her breast that read, "Ute Mountain Utes: 100 years and still dancing."

The next morning, a pink sunrise over Mesa Verde cast a soft and rosy blanket on the Sleeping Ute. As the sun slipped down the side, it illuminated the cracks and humps, the details of the mountain. Down in Towaoc it did the same.

Charles Knight saddled his white Appaloosa and went looking for fifty mohair goats, missing on the mountain.

Carl readied a corral and loading chute near Navajo Springs. The cattle would be coming down from the high country soon, to winter pasture.

Kate entered the hospital to have a gall bladder operation.

And Judy got Gerrael off to Head Start before heading for her office to wrestle with declining revenues from oil wells.

As fall began, life on the Ute Mountain Reservation returned to normal.

The dancing was over.

9

A Community of Contradictions

*T*he roads that lead to the Ute reservation descend from the mountains like streams, cutting through both values and time. Driving them in autumn is a melancholy trip. From present to past and forward again. They begin in the high country where aspens glow richest. Life is good there. The Utes knew that, once upon a time. They summered, hunted and left each fall when snow began to dust the peaks. A century ago, they exited for good, forced by white miners to the south and west. The roads today follow their footsteps out of the mountains, descending, retreating, to the reservation in the far-off corner of Colorado.

"This whole place was Ute territory," said Carl Knight, waving his arm at the end of the trail. "From Santa Fe to the Wyoming state line. All the mountain country." He stood at the foot of Ute Mountain as a band of wild horses galloped by, heading west toward the Utah line. His wave took in most of Colorado—and much of his family's life. "I can still remember what my grandmother said. They got pushed out of there."

Carl is a descendant of the Weeminuche, one of seven bands of Utes. When the Spaniards first saw them in the 1600s, the Utes numbered about 4,000 and roamed most of the state, from the Front Range west. The Weeminuche kept mostly to the San Juan Basin. But old pictures show Carl's grandmother in the Valley of the Gods outside Colorado Springs.

When the Spaniards deeded the Southwest to the United States in 1848, the Anglos immediately tried to contain the Indians. The first treaty, in 1849, required them to "cease the roving and rambling habits which have hitherto marked them as a people." That roaming, though, left a legacy on the landscape: musical words of description—Saguache, for spring in blue earth; Cochetopa, for buffalo pass; Pagosa Springs, healing waters; Uncompahgre, the red lake. The old words rumbled in Carl's throat.

I'd first heard them in the high country, near Gunnison and Crested Butte where I'd spent the spring writing about ranching. The area was rich with Ute history. Even the cattle were there, originally, to feed the Indians.

But that was 100 years ago. Little was known about the modern Utes. Yet I considered them, along with rancher-cowboys, to be the classic characters of the West—wrapped mostly in myth. Like the cowboys, the Indians deserved a sympathetic and honest portrayal. I asked Carl Knight and members of his family to let me write about them. With some hesitation, they agreed. To reach them, I traveled from Gunnison down the old trails, across the passes and beyond the San Juans, just as Carl's people had done.

The land changed dramatically as it dropped from steep wet forests with running streams to irrigated homesteads carved from rolling sagebrush around Durango, Mancos and Cortez. Apple trees red with fruit grew along the highways. Hay was being baled in adjacent fields. Then the land flattened. The green-topped mesas sloughed to a Mancos shale, dry and dusty. Rabbit brush bloomed yellow on a desert landscape. To the west, Ute Mountain lay colored in the autumn sun. Beyond, to the south, in a wide-open range, I met Carl.

Built like a bull rider, at home on a horse, Carl is director of Ute Mountain natural resources—the ranches and roads on the half-million acres of reservation land. "I've built roads where people haven't been," he said. "I lived in a tent. I lived in a hogan. I lived in a dugout that's still sitting by that store." He pointed east toward Mancos Creek. Another group of horses galloped by. "We used to rope 'em wild and saddle them."

Carl and his siblings were raised in a horse-and-buggy era by a grandmother named Amy Kent Snow. In the winter she lived in a hogan on a mesa, a place Carl called home. "My first memory—when I came to my senses—was looking up at a horse. I had a horse that was given to me. Friday evening after school I'd hit the trail and I'd ride across that desert, down to Mancos Creek, to be with my grandmother. There's a horse trail that leads up that mesa. Sunday evening or Monday morning, I'd hit the trail again."

In the tents and hogans she lived in, Grandma Snow passed on a family history that the Knights still recite: "Everywhere the white men went, they took the best land," said Carl. Twenty years after gold was discovered in Cherry Creek in 1858 and Denver was founded on the spot, white men had climbed into the mountains and, by incremental treaties, pushed the Utes out. First from the Front Range, then the San Juans, then after the Ute slaying of agent Nathan Meeker on the White River, out of the mountains completely.

"My grandmother was at Meeker at the time," said Carl. "They scattered in little bunches. Somehow or other she ended up at Silverton. She used to tell me. The cavalry came in. The white settlers came in, in bunches. They had found a shiny piece of rock."

* * *

If left to statistics, the Utes of Ute Mountain would have withered like annuals in a desert frost. So dismal are the facts that they hide the spirit of the reservation, growing from a perennial taproot of forbearance. The same is true of first impressions. I first saw the reservation under a blazing sun in a summer drought that yellowed even irrigated fields. Where the water ended and the reservation began, the land was held down, it seemed, by weeds.

The village of Towaoc, fifteen miles south of Cortez, is surrounded by scrubland on a bench beneath the Sleeping Ute. The blacktop road to it climbs a hill toward the mountain's "toe," a volcanic cone. Set back from the road on either side are home lots scattered in the sage and rabbit brush. There are split-level homes of cream and brown and run-down bungalows of fading pink. New cars, junkers, lawns and bare ground surround the houses along with Chinese elm, a tree that thrives here.

Past Arrow Head Street, Red Horse Turn and Whispering Wind Drive, the road crests. The post office is on the right, the police station on the left. The only store is closed, the gas pumps empty. Straight ahead is the year-old tribal headquarters, adobe and circular and painted tan, surrounded by thick lawn.

Beyond that, the old village square is lined with government-issue buildings from 1918. It looks like a cavalry post, but the U.S. flag instead flies over the Bureau of Indian Affairs, housed in a one-time dormitory of a boarding school. Next to it is Head Start.

Paved streets lead away to homes to the north. Their names ring of Ute history and natural sights: Chief House Street, North Star Lane. At the far end of Rustling Willow Street, many of the Knight clan reside: Kate, the grandmother in a small house; Gladys Hammond in a two-story suburban; and Gladys's children and grandchildren in a house and trailer next door.

Not far away, in a yellow ranch house, Judy Knight lives with husband Bob Frank. I found them outside at sunset, eating supper on TV tables, facing east toward Mesa Verde. From Judy's lawn overlooking the village, I could see an abandoned house, a car on its rims, more weeds scattered between lots. But I could also see Judy's border of flowers, a bushy willow shading her lawn, a family at home in the evening. Down her driveway, past the car with flat tires, Gerrael pedaled a Big Wheel.

The impression depended on where I looked. The picture demanded a choice of focus. But where?

Statistically, the Ute Mountain reservation ranks among the poorest in the United States. There is 57 percent unemployment and a 69 percent school dropout rate. Forty-seven percent of the 1,600 people are below the poverty level, and life expectancy is thirty-eight years. "If you looked at the statistics, you'd think you have a whole lot of sad people and a sad situation," said Bob. "[But] a lot of people are pretty satisfied."

The same contradiction occurs in the large Knight family. Largely educated, savvy and holding key jobs on the reservation, there also is alcoholism, joblessness and death at an early age. Judy pointed to an old mobile home nearby, used for drinking parties by a niece she had raised. Police had been called to break them up. "I wonder where I went wrong," said Judy. But the Knights' focus is life, not death. Hope, not hopelessness. "We have problems, and we are working on them," Judy said.

Terry, Judy's brother, is another statistic. He is out of a job because of tribal budget cutbacks. He hocked his .270 Weatherby hunting rifle for enough gas to go to a sun dance. But seeing him as a number means failing to appreciate the person, the spiritual leader, a man who can joke about his need for cash, then pray for the elders. "I was taught to keep my head above water," he said, stretching his neck. "Like the swan—head up, looking good, but below water you're kicking like crazy."

Nor could a statistic capture the spirit of Sunday afternoons at Gladys's house. The family cooks outdoors on an oak fire and eats around the big living room, playing with the children and watching HBO. Gladys has survived her husband's death from lung cancer and a boy's suicide. She has four grown children living at her home. Three others live next door and come over Sunday with their families. In addition, Gladys is caring for Kate, who is recuperating from her gallstone operation, and two-year-old Lisa, a foster child from a broken home elsewhere on the reservation.

While *Gorillas in the Mist* played on TV, Gladys knelt by the outside fire and patted tortillas into shape. Daughter-in-law Laura, who is white, grilled ribs. The grandkids played with a pack of dogs.

"How many dogs do you have?" I asked.

"Too many," someone said.

Just then a puppy grabbed a rib from a plate and ran. Everyone hooted. Someone mentioned a food truck due from Phoenix. Safeway sends outdated Twinkies, fruits and canned goods to the reservation once a month. "Oh, we can eat again," said Gladys. It was a joke. No one goes hungry in her family.

In my first few days with the Knights the choice of focus faded as an issue. On a reservation burdened by statistics, their humor and perseverance impressed me. I could point to no more poignant example than watching Charles Knight, on a blistering day, water a willow in hardscrabble ground. I helped him haul water in a tank from Judy's house to his trailer, two miles south of Towaoc. He backed the truck to two little trees nearly lost in the landscape. The willows had come from Judy's tree, the one in her yard, and Charles's attitude about them said all I needed to know about spirit versus statistics.

As the water disappeared in the dry old shale, the old man said: "It's going to grow big. Then I'll put grass under it. Sit under it. Just like Judy's."

Charles Knight sat alone on Ute Mountain in a folding chair, scanning for goats. His gnarled hands held binoculars. One of his dogs nuzzled into them, and Charles spoke to him quietly in Ute. Fifty white mohair goats, his entire herd, were missing on the mountain, and Charles was worried, a little angry. He scoped the thick scrub oak and spoke again. "I can't make it up the mountain. Used to, when I was young."

A sheep baaed from a pen nearby. Two white Appaloosa horses stood in a corral. Charles sat in the shade of a piñon tree at his sheep camp beneath the crossed arms of the Sleeping Ute. Behind him the Montezuma valley lay clear to the La Plata Mountains.

"Maybe they up top," Charles said. His hands traced a trail to the summit. "I ride every day, every day. That's why I lose weight. Other people you see, they eat eat eat. They fat. They don't work. I work hard. I growed that way, Indian way." He laughed and showed a stub of a tooth. The dentist had pulled one the day before, and his gum was sore.

"That's why I never do anything. I never drink. I never smoke. That's why I'm here."

Fence rider, rodeo competitor and livestock producer, Charles belies nearly every white impression about Indians. Measured in the old Ute way, he is a rich man. He has a few horses, a few dozen cows, sheep—and fifty goats, somewhere. "I take goats to trading post in Navajo, Mohair. Get check. Maybe $250, $400."

But livestock is his only income. He gets no social security—and no monthly check from the government. "My father, if he didn't have livestock, would be on welfare," said Judy. "A government check? I wish I got one. Most of them think we get money just for being Indian."

Between the 1890s, when they were herded onto their reservation, until the 1930s, the Utes got rations from the government—salt and beans, basically. They were a remnant of nineteenth-century treaties, handed out by government agents to make up for lost land where the Utes had fed and clothed themselves. The rations were to continue until the Indians were "capable of sustaining themselves." Other provisions ranged from "one gentle American cow, as distinguished from the ordinary Mexican or Texas breed," to school and a blacksmith, to $25,000 a year "forever."

But between 1931, when rations stopped, and 1950, most families survived on livestock, the Knights among them. "Prior to the '50s, we didn't have any money," said Judy. "My family worked in the beanfields in Dove Creek. We lived in tents."

From his mountain perch, Charles waved his brown hand to show where tents sat scattered on the land. "Teepees. Here, there."

In 1950 the tribe received $6 million in a lawsuit over lost treaty land and gave much of it to individuals. Families received $3,000 per person under tribal-approved "family plans," which allowed the building of houses and the purchase of furniture, vehicles and livestock. The families began to gather in Towaoc, a Ute word used to answer greetings. It means "O.K." or "All right." There the Knights built their first frame home, which Kate still occupies.

Additional per capita money was put in a trust for the children. When Judy was eighteen she received $1,800, which she spent on furniture and cattle. Terry, her younger brother, received $5,300 because of growth in the investment. He split it with his mother and took his share to college. Some of his fellow teenagers, he said, bought a car and lots of beer with their "eighteen money."

In the mid-1950s, oil, gas and uranium were discovered on the reservation, and the tribe used royalties to run its government and give more per capita payments. That arrangement remains today. The tribal budget of $2.6 million—most of it salaries for 247 people—comes from mineral royalties on the reservation. Because royalties dropped dramatically in the 1980s, the per capita payment this year is $500.

An additional $2.2 million in federal money is spent by the Bureau of Indian Affairs for services that stem from the treaties. About half of that is for social services such as the placement of foster children and "GA," general assistance. About 300 adults and children out of the tribe's 1,600 receive welfare, similar to welfare payments anywhere, either from the tribe's GA account or Montezuma County's Aid to Families with Dependent Children. The payments range from $41 a week for a single person with no rent to $76 for a mother with three children.

There are many people, including Terry, who feel that per capita payments led to a welfare mentality on the reservation. "These people got spoiled when they got all those millions. Now they still want it, and there's no money," he said.

The Knights, each of them with a few head of livestock from Charles's original herd and most with jobs, appear affluent by comparison. Judy makes $24,000 a year as vice-chairman of the tribe. Like any American, she pays federal income tax.

"I've never been on welfare," she said. "I was out of a job once. I had five kids to feed. I just found work. I've always worked." It was a lesson learned from Charles. "I've always seen him working—and we had to help. He'd tell us once. If you were asked again, you were sorry you were asked."

Charles got up to saddle a horse and look along the roads for his goats. "I used to be really good riding broncos.

They don't throw me off," he said. He raised his hands to imaginary reins. "You watch the head, which way he's going to jump. He go straight, he's not strong. Some horses twist this way, make you crazy." He laughed again and headed down the road with his dogs beside him. "I still riding the horses."

10

Square Houses, Round Lives

"*A*re you going to get old in office?" the woman yelled at Judy Knight. "Your time is up!"

"Where's all the money?" someone barked at another council member. "The tribe doesn't tell us anything."

"Are you going to fire everyone?" asked a third person from the crowd. "You guys turn us away like a dog."

Judy, dressed in jeans and boots, leaned against a lunch table and listened. Then she spoke back sharply in Ute. "If all the things I've done for you aren't enough, if you don't have any confidence in me, I have no business here."

In a school cafeteria, Judy and the three other candidates for tribal chairman stood before the dreaded Nuche— "the people," the source of their power and punishment. It was a candid exchange. "You have to have a tough hide," Judy said later. After ten years on the council, two as chairman and the last three as vice-chairman, she was reaping a familiar refrain from voters. It's time for a change. In a week Judy and the other candidates would put their necks on the voting block.

The election process is exactly like ours, right down to charges of vote-buying, rumor-mongering and nepotism. Amplified by the small-town nature of a reservation, the campaign is proof that in the last fifty years Indians have learned our system of politics all too well. "We get involved in your national politics, too," said Judy, who worked on Gary Hart's campaign for president. "I know how important national politics is to Indian tribes. We have to educate Washington on what we need."

The Weeminuche band, which makes up the Ute Mountain Ute tribe, became a constitutional democracy in 1940 after eons of life under chiefs, chosen for their wisdom or prowess. The last traditional chief, Jack House, remained influential until his death in 1971. His grandson, Ernest House, is chairman today. He sits across from a bronze statue of his grandfather in the council chambers.

Under the tribal constitution, the seven-member council is all powerful. It manages virtually every aspect of reservation life, from animal herds to jobs to "relief" for tribal members. Relief means help ranging from rides to cash to funeral arrangements. The old paternalistic practice of the tribe taking care of its members remains.

"I would love to run the tribe as a business, but there is no way to do it," said Judy. "The council has always taken care of them. How do you get them past that? A lot of people think being on council is fun and games. You get in there and get paid and travel. That's a bunch of bull. This job is just like a big family with all these kids relying on you."

Just as in national politics, no one talks about cutting pork during an election campaign. Just the opposite. "I promise to cut council salaries and use it for jobs," said Gerald Peabody, the tribe's housing director and one of Judy's opponents for chairman. "I'll do away with time clocks" and trust people to do their jobs, promised Nelson Elkriver, a councilman and rodeo competitor running for chairman. His trademark is a big black hat. The fourth candidate, Carl Cuthair, vowed to improve education and economics on the reservation.

Terry Knight is one of eleven candidates vying for three other seats on the tribal council. Terry served several years before, including one term as chairman. At the crowded candidate's night meeting he spoke in Ute, promising jobs, education, an open government and good times ahead, thanks to new federal economic development funds. "This tribe will be sitting on plenty of money," he said.

Nearly every candidate was asked if he would fire existing staff. The tribe is the reservation's biggest employer, with 247 people, and councilmen are influential in placing another 200 jobs with the Bureau of Indian Affairs and various tribal enterprises.

Ten years ago job security was the issue that swept Judy Knight into office. At the time, job security was nil. Each new administration brought new faces. During her ten years, Judy created a personnel policy with a grievance procedure. Now she has the trappings of the vice-chairman: an office, a travel allowance and a steady trickle of constituents asking for help. On nearly every working day they come to her on the second floor of the tribal headquarters, and she fits them in between other duties.

Judy's campaigning is low-key. She printed one flyer listing her accomplishments, but she prefers personal visits. At the Bear Dance she talked with people. She attended a fall picnic near White Mesa. She eats lunch regularly with senior citizens. After ten years in politics, she recognizes a photo opportunity, whether a camera is there or not. "There's still more things to do," she said. "There are a lot of things you can't do unless you're at the top."

Today, Columbus Day, though, don't expect to find Judy or any of the tribal officials at work. As much as the Utes joke about Columbus and his "discovery" of Indians in the

New World—"We should have sent him back," is one line— they relish the day set aside in his honor.

Government employees—even in Indian country— love three-day weekends.

Within a few steps of Terry Knight's door are symbols of his medicine. Teepee poles and canvas, a sweat lodge, a shade house, a hogan—traditional structures of Indian life. Terry spends a part of each week in them.

But when a group of Japanese tourists paid a call, they found him inside his $60,000 split-level home, the one with air conditioning on the south wall and a carport so filled with dirt bikes, chain saws and lawn chairs that his pickup sits outside. "I think they were disappointed in me," said Terry. "The medicine man is supposed to be poor and dirty and have limited use of English. He doesn't watch MTV and doesn't drink Corona. They expected to see me in buckskin with a skull on the TV."

What they may have seen on the TV was one of the rented videos he often plays. When I rang the doorbell and walked in, it was some awful caveman movie with Ringo Starr. Terry was only half-watching from the dining room table as he wrapped leather around feathers for an upcoming ceremony. Flaydina, his wife, and their infant, Tawnie Snow, nuzzled quietly on the couch. *World Book* volumes filled one shelf and totems another. Buffalo and eagle carvings lay everywhere. "I think I'm the link between the old and the new," he said.

But Terry has to work at it. He believes that houses like his, a rust-colored six-bedroom model built with HUD money in 1979, are breaking down old values. Most traditional Indian structures are round—the sacred circle of their belief system. What goes around comes around. But almost all Indians now live in square houses lined up on streets, a pattern that erodes the Indian's relationship with the land and his extended family. "The Indian and the land are one," he said. "If I could, I would stand in the ground halfway to my knees, and you could see that."

Terry's house is away from town, a few hundred yards from Mesa Verde. When he walks outside his house, he sees earth and sky, not another house. He was raised that way, and his spiritual work is rooted in it. "Living like the white man, you're not out in the environment. If you're lining up everyone the same, it changes something inside you."

Until the 1950s, most of the Ute Mountain Utes lived in traditional houses such as tents and hogans. Treaty settlement money allowed families to build the first conventional homes. Terry's mother's house, built in the 1950s, was one of the first on the reservation with running water. Twenty years later, in 1976, HUD began building small, $36,000 homes scattered around the village. Terry's sister, Judy, bought one and moved in with five children.

Since 1982 Towaoc has received a steady flow of new HUD homes, which, for cost and utility efficiency, were built along straight lines on the north side of town. As a result, Towaoc has the appearance, in places, of a rapidly growing development.

At the request of the housing director, Terry blessed the new houses; this week he performed special prayers prior to ground-breaking for units being built near an Anasazi ruin. Dressed in his jeans and cowboy shirt, Terry built a fire and burned cedar and herbs near the old kiva wall, a round ceremonial chamber used about A.D. 1000. "I talked to the old Anasazi spirits and told them we're going to be building new homes, and not to let the machinery and people disrupt them. I told them families would be living there. I asked them to be more like a guardian force."

Had Terry not "balanced" the area, Ute families would have been reluctant to move in, said Gerald Peabody, the housing director. Those who did "most likely would be haunted and not sleep too good," said Terry.

The Ute Mountain Ute tribal housing department, considered the worst managed in the Rocky Mountain region six years ago, is now ranked first by HUD in Denver. There are 150 relatively new HUD homes, with another seventy-seven rental units. They cost the government $13.3 million. Another 100 families live in older homes and trailers, and there is a waiting list for another fifty-six.

The HUD owners pay according to income. Terry, currently unemployed, pays $50 a month. Judy, with two incomes, pays $300. In twenty-five years, the homes will be theirs. They take pride in ownership. Judy has remodeled and landscaped extensively, and HUD used her house in a video on Indian housing.

But property ownership is a relatively recent notion to the Ute Mountain Utes. No one "owns" the reservation; it is common ground. The result is that some people consider their tenure in the HUD homes as only temporary, said Terry. It shows in upkeep, exacerbated by poor-quality construction and the lack of remodeling funds.

Terry makes it a point to spend time in traditional Indian structures. Once a week he leads a sweat, a sauna-like ceremony with hot rocks and water conducted in a low cloth-covered dome. He invited me to attend that evening, but I declined. "Too bad," he answered. "The members were looking forward to seeing the white man we were going to sacrifice."

Terry also leads services of the Native American Church, which uses peyote as a sacrament in an all-night ceremony. A teepee is used, about the only time a teepee is seen on the reservation. "We have to be one in two worlds. Half the kids don't have the outdoor skills I grew up with. They know how to run a VCR. The life-style is changing."

He told Ute students recently: "Old people—their purpose in life was to survive. You've got it made. You don't have to starve, to hunt, to go on raids. You can sleep 'til noon and not worry about someone coming to get your hair."

But such a life-style forgets the Indian's connection with the land. "After a while we'll all live like white men. We'll live in a square house and pay mortgages and live by the golden dollar."

The coffee pot is bottomless at the home of Gladys Knight Hammond, filled with a rich, black blend that never hints at the effort behind it. From somewhere in the kitchen, it just keeps coming, cup after cup.

"This is good," I said, sipping. "So, what's the problem with the water?"

"Try it," said Gladys from her perch on the couch.

Becky, her daughter, turned the faucet on and handed me a glassful. "Pretend it's wine," she said.

The bouquet struck as I raised the glass. I took a swallow. It tasted as bad as it smelled. I went back to the coffee.

"We never drink water out of a faucet," said Brenda, thirty-one, another daughter. "It gives you the runs."

For as long as she can remember, Brenda's family has driven as far for coffee water as it has for coffee—to Cortez, fifteen miles away. Once every two weeks, no matter the weather, they've taken big cans to town, filled them at a city pump or a relative's hose and hauled them home. The four fifty-gallon Gott jugs are kept below the stairs in the basement, along with half a dozen smaller containers. "The fun part is carrying them upstairs," said Becky.

The water is used for cooking and drinking. Grandchildren in the family learn early not to play with the push-button nozzle. "You don't waste it," said Gladys. "It's a long haul."

Long haul, indeed. Since 1868, the Ute Mountain Utes have had untreated, inadequate or unsafe water. This fall, that will change. In a pipe and canal being built from the McPhee Reservoir twenty-five miles away, good water will start to flow to the reservation. Already, drinking water is headed to Towaoc. Irrigation water will take a few years.

If Congress pays the full $73 million tab, the project will bring enough water to the reservation to irrigate 8,000 acres of desert, put Utes to work farming and make obsolete the endemic orange jugs that sit on every porch, kitchen counter and pickup truck on the reservation.

The drinking water will be available in homes next month, but it will be hard to change habits. The water now running in Towaoc pipes comes from the tail-end of an irrigation canal, laced with salt, herbicides, dung and silt. It is poured through a bed of sand and given a healthy shot of chlorine to kill the biggest bugs. Still, lab tests sometimes come back with the bacteria marked "too numerous to count." "I won't drink it," said Terry McClain, the tribe's public works director. He put "Do Not Drink" signs over the brand-new fountains at tribal headquarters.

The hard water has ruined two water heaters at Judy Knight's, made grandson Garrael sick, stained the toilets at Terry's, spotted cars all over town and turned white the brown paint on tribal headquarters where the lawn sprinklers splashed the building. Little wonder Gladys says of the new water: "I'm afraid to try it. Around Christmas, maybe."

The Ute Mountain water story reads like so many chapters in Indian history. "It's criminal," said John Porter, the man in charge of delivering 23,000 acre-feet of water from McPhee Reservoir to the reservation by the mid-1990s. It's also the story of strange bedfellows—white bean farmers and Indians—using each other to overcome congressional resistance to big water projects.

The Indians had water rights but needed Bureau of Reclamation projects to get the water. They got it by piggybacking onto two nearby federal projects, Animas–La Plata near Durango and the Dolores project near Cortez. Both are multimillion-dollar irrigation projects that environmentalists call wasteful pork barrels.

The McPhee Reservoir is part of the Dolores project and will supply the first water to the Ute Mountain Utes. If the Animas-La Plata project is completed, the Utes would get still more water. "There would not have been either the Dolores or the Animas–La Plata without the Indians," said Porter.

There was strong resistance to the projects in the U.S. Senate until Judy Knight described the horrible drinking water and showed pictures of elders on the parched reservation, according to state Attorney General Duane Woodard. "It was a poignant moment when she described to Senator Dan Inouye how the only dependable, potable water supply had to come from Cortez by truck. He was deeply touched."

Woodard got involved in negotiations because water rights are settled in state courts, and because he grew up in Cortez. He saw racism firsthand: merchants overcharging Indians and segregation in bars and motels. Woodard was instrumental in bringing together white farmers and Indians after years of ignorance and bigotry on both sides.

For a time during discussions, farmers didn't even want to share the same canal with "Indian" water. But the tribe had law on its side—a 1908 federal court ruling that reservations must have water to make them fertile. It also gave tribes water rights that dated to the creation of their reservation. In the case of the Ute Mountain Utes, that meant 1868, a time when the Animas, La Plata, Dolores, Mancos and San Juan rivers flowed unimpeded across Indian land.

Insolent or ignorant of that ruling, white men dammed and diverted the rivers. The Mancos River, which cuts the Ute Mountain land, "used to flow a bunch," said Carl Knight, who grew up in a dugout house cut in its banks.

After the federal government dammed the river upstream for the Mancos ranching community in the 1940s, the river dried up on the reservation.

To pay for that transgression, Uncle Sam agreed in the recent settlement to build a canal to the Ute Mountain Ute Reservation and spend $32 million to develop farmland. The state agreed to pay $6 million for a drinking water pipeline. Another $34 million is needed finally to grow crops with center-pivot irrigation systems southwest of Ute Mountain. Longer-range plans, requiring more millions from Congress, would irrigate an additional 12,000 acres in the Mancos River area.

The millions will generate jobs, necessary on a reservation with finite coal and oil reserves, said Judy, who led tribal negotiations. Already, an experimental farm near Towaoc is being run by tribal trainees in anticipation of a big farm in the 1990s. The farm would grow wheat, corn, beans and alfalfa and employ fifty people during peak times.

To build roads, power lines and sprinklers, the federal government will pay $3,000 to $5,000 an acre, a figure some might consider uneconomical.

But, said Judy, "No amount of money will make up for 120 years without water."

11

Why Do People Have Different Color Skin?

*T*he attack began at dawn, deep in Indian territory. As the troops emerged from their tents, the volleys began.

"Was that you snoring?"

"Was it the governor?"

"Don't blame me. I could hear it three tents away."

The governor's staff huddled by the fire and grumbled in their coffee. It was a chilly morning on the Ute Mountain Ute Reservation and the nonsnorers were cranky.

"What a way to get to know the attorney general," said Fred Neihaus, director of Colorado's business development. "Waiting in a teepee together for daybreak."

In a retreat from their gold-plated tower in Denver, Governor Roy Romer's cabinet was getting to know one another—intimately. Camped in five teepees along the Mancos River, they saw their fat, foibles and fiber.

"The danger in politics is not dealing with the real world," said Romer. "Out in the country ... everybody has about the same reach getting up a cliff. You get a more truthful measure of who you are, and that's very important if you lead."

For three days the governor and his staff toured Anasazi ruins throughout the 125,000-acre tribal park adjacent to Mesa Verde National Park. They bathed in the muddy river, they ate on hay bales and they told campfire stories beneath a full moon. They also learned something about the Utes and the reservation—a foreign land to them.

"You're getting to be a regular Anasazi, governor," said park supervisor Arthur Cuthair as Romer, sixty-one, scrambled down a rock face from a cliffside dwelling.

"That means the ancient one, right?" quipped Morgan Smith, director of international trade.

Cuthair led the group up narrow rock ladders, through pine woods, along slick-rock cliffs. On one, a tarantula stopped the group. "The Utes say where the tarantula goes, a deer will follow," said Cuthair. At times the group leaped ten centuries in seconds as the governor radioed instructions for a National Guard deployment near Glenwood Springs, then felt his way down 1,000-year-old steps carved in sandstone. Emerging from an ancient ceremonial kiva, staffers called for the score of the University of Colorado football game being played that moment in Boulder.

"There's a bond you reach here that goes beyond the working one," said Romer. He mentioned Melanie Vogl, an assistant who had gone on two previous retreats. She had died of cancer in July. In her last days, Romer and his staff had been her family, the office her hospice. "There is a quality that we're after here, described in that experience," he said. "You don't get that possibility unless you know people well enough to be vulnerable."

Later, around a campfire, he mulled the Anasazi family structure and the need for families in a society that breaks them down. They are crucial, he said, to problems of drug abuse and education. "What is the form of the tribe in our society?" asked Romer. "Is it IBM? It is, in part. We can't go back to the tribe. But we need to find new institutional ways to organize the community."

Romer and his staff, a group of strong individuals, had come here in search of a community. But the place they had chosen to look, the Ute Mountain Ute Reservation, was diametrically occupied—it is a community of people struggling to be individuals.

The Indians are foremost members of a tribe. But the U.S. system of government and economics is rooted in individualism, not tribalism. In every facet of tribal life— politics, government, family, jobs—there is an almost daily conflict between the two forms of society. Young adults must decide between their extended families and leaving the reservation for decent-paying jobs. The tribal council walks a line between paternalism to members and white man's accountability. Social workers, acting on behalf of an Indian child's rights, place him in a foster home outside of the tribal cocoon.

"The problem with a lot of people is the way the tribe was set up a long time ago," said Judy Knight. "The head of the tribe took care of things. Today, everybody should be accountable. Some think Indians don't have to be. Their ideas are from years ago."

Even living in a HUD home, paying a mortgage, is a tiny breakdown of tribal life. "In a sense, we're losing our identity by being accountable," said Gerald Peabody, the tribe's housing director. "Being acculturated takes a lot away from being an Indian. But how can we not be more like a white man and compete in the modern world?"

Ironically, and sadly, what Governor Romer and his staff were looking for in the reservation retreat is what the Utes, in their pursuit of the American dream, are losing.

* * *

Judy Knight's sofa looks a bit like her desk—piled with work. Oil contracts on one, ironing on the other; federal regulations, and beading. Pink call-back slips, and pink cereal dropped by her grandson. In another culture she might be called superwoman. In hers, it's just Judy. "We were taught to carry our own, whether chasing horses or whatever had to be done," she said. "Everybody had a job."

Judy's job in another month will be to lead the Ute Mountain Ute tribe into the 1990s. She was elected chairman last week, and she takes office November 3. It is a daunting task, given the economic and social problems of the reservation. But it is one that Judy Knight has been in training for nearly all her forty-six years. "My father always said, 'Do whatever you do the best you can. Think for yourself. Think ahead.'"

Judy was born when most Utes could think no farther ahead than their next meal. The reservation was isolated by miles and neglect. The Bureau of Indian Affairs had just closed its office on the reservation, requiring eighty-five miles of travel to Ignacio for any government services. She went to boarding school in Ignacio, where Ute language and culture were discouraged. She came of age while the U.S. government was trying to "terminate" Indian tribes by dissolving their status as sovereign nations. In the mid-1960s, she and her first husband became part of a relocation project aimed at moving Indians to cities "to start living the way everybody else does." They moved to California, and she worked for Aetna Insurance.

As a result Judy today carries with her, not far below the surface, an anger over U.S. policies. She speaks of broken 100-year-old treaties as if she had been lied to personally. "When you go off the reservation to live, you get shot," she said once, as if it still happened. She was referring to the massacre of a Ute hunting party by cowboys near Dolores—in 1885.

Judy heard such stories from elders. Her education has been both traditional and mainstream. She learned the Sun Dance and accounting. She speaks Ute and the language of lawyers. "I am an Indian, but I've got to deal with the non-Indian way of life. I need both to be balanced."

Like many Indians, Judy is shy on first meeting and avoids eye-to-eye contact. When she trusts, or gets riled, she looks directly and speaks her mind. She can be brutally blunt, even about family matters. "My kids are no different than the rest of them around here," she said. "The girl (twenty-year-old daughter Lee Ann) did fine in school. She got some training. [But] she doesn't want to work. She doesn't want to take care of her kid. Where did she get that? She says it's my fault."

Her personal life became part of her election campaign when anonymous literature circulated that suggested Judy had enriched herself from tribal coffers. It mentioned race horses and Porsches. She answered directly. She does own riding horses—from her dad's herd—and once owned a Porsche, thanks to an uncle's inheritance. Now she had a red Chevy convertible. "I always wanted a convertible. I'm like everybody else."

Judy raised five children—three of them belonging to a sister killed in a car wreck—while working full-time. Eleven years ago, when they were teenagers, she ran for the council, a job that has occupied her since. "When I got on council, I really didn't know anything. One thing I've learned—it never hurts to ask or put anything forward."

With a gift for figures—Judy wants to be a CPA someday—she tackled mineral leases and water law. "I didn't know what an acre-foot was. I just knew we didn't have it." She surrounded herself with expert staff, many of them white. Mike Preston, for example, helped negotiate the water deal that will bring good water to the reservation for the first time. "I'd say to Mike, 'I know nothing. Teach me.'"

Her knowledge, combined with her subsurface indignation, made her an effective negotiator in Washington.

For ten years she also has represented the tribe on the Council of Energy Resource Tribes, or CERT, a Denver organization which gives technical advice to Indian tribes on oil, coal and gas leases. She was reelected chairwoman last month, a position held in the past by Peter MacDonald, the Navajo leader, and Ross Swimmer, who went on to become assistant interior secretary. With ideas generated at CERT, Judy helped negotiate oil and gas leases on the Ute Mountain Reservation that require companies to hire Utes and investment in a fund that will continue annual per capita cash payments to tribal members.

But along the way she has also grown increasingly frustrated with a tribal mentality rooted in old ways. "The per capita payment is not good for the people. But it's their money. People still feel when you get on the council you are there to help them, and that can mean anything. The constitution says we have to live with family problems."

Her biggest challenge as chairman is to break the welfare mentality, to create enough jobs to support families, a task she faces with typical bluntness. "Even if we create jobs, some people won't work," she said. "It's frustrating." At times, in fact, it's impossible to separate the burdens of the reservation "family" from Judy's own. Members come to her house for help, sometimes seeking handouts of money. It is a custom, and she obliges when she can.

She also plans to adopt grandson Gerrael, a rambunctious three-year-old who gives her both pleasure and headaches. Adoption will take custody away from her daughter to create a stable home life for the boy. But he is often demanding—earlier this week she had to take him along when she met Governor Roy Romer.

Little wonder that when she seeks some escape, she leaves the reservation for dinner with her husband or reads after Gerrael is in bed.

"It gets my mind off things and keeps me from going crazy," she said. "I guess it's like therapy." When she reads, she turns to novels by Sidney Sheldon or Tony Hillerman. "I'm not too crazy about real life stories."

Even at noon, the sun on Blue Mesa cast long, cold shadows filled with frost. The ranch hands wore their gloves, and Carl Knight, supervising from atop a rail, was bundled thick in a canvas vest. "It gives me a sad feeling when fall comes on," he said. "You know how winter is. There are people that can't cope with it."

Below him, his boys and other members of the Ute tribe chased calves down an alley, trying to spot a brand. They had to rope every tenth one or so to allow the brand inspector to take a closer look and determine its owner. "It's their life, some of these guys," said Carl.

Every fall, chief cowboy Carl Knight pulls together the cattle from six ranches owned by the Ute Mountain Ute tribe and holds a calf sale. From 30,000 acres of high country rangeland off the reservation, 700 calves were on the block this year. It's a community sale—an annual gathering of thirty-eight brands and their families. Part business, part ritual, the sale is an autumn rite for the Utes. "Cattle are a traditional way of life for the Utes," Carl said.

The auction is held at Pinecrest Ranch, 18,479 acres on Blue Mesa near Gunnison. It is high country, 8,500 feet, where the fall breezes never quite lose their morning chill. Carl wore a hat, a thick shirt and work boots. A turquoise bandana wrapped his throat. The vest made his thick chest even bigger.

The calves bawled for their mothers. The cows grazed near tree line—a bunch of aspen shorn of their leaves. Uncompahgre Peak, to the south, wore a snow cap in a sky full of blue. "If that white stuff gets down here, we'll have to move out of here," said Carl.

As the tribal director of natural resources, Carl runs cattle for tribal members on ranches purchased mainly with oil and gas receipts during the 1950s and 1960s. They are owned for the benefit of tribal members who raise livestock. Those include the Knights: Carl, Charles—with 100 head—and Judy and Terry, who have a handful.

The cow owners get nearly all the receipts from the sale—this year $360 for a 400-pound calf. Over twenty years, weights of the calves have gone up 100 pounds, thanks to better breeding. "It's not just a job, it's my land," said Carl. "And these cows that belong to members, they're mine. I've got to take care of them as if they belonged to me."

Of all the Knights, Carl is the one said by family members to be most "Indian." He is remote, tied to values and images from another time. "Fall," he said, "it gives me a feeling way down inside. Winter is coming on. The old people used to get ready for winter. They got their dried meat stocked, they got their vegetables dried. They fixed up their house. They had to have feed for their animals. This life that was given to me, it blends in with the rest of creation. I don't fight Mother Nature. I try to live with her."

As he talked, children in a small corral wrestled with three calves found without brands. They chased and bull-dogged to the laughter from chute roosters who watched from the rail. Patrick, Carl's boy, applied the iron.

Tribal children used to have 4-H projects and take cattle to the National Western Stock Show in Denver. "They don't do that any more," said Carl. "Too much TV. Fancy cars. What you call heavy metal. It's too much for my ears. I like to get out there in the fresh air, no pollution. You can hear those elk bugling."

Carl was raised by a grandmother he adored, but at age seven was taken from her. "They called it school. Boarding school. The only thing I knew how to say in English was 'my friend.' I just got lonely. They told me how to run a broom, a mop. You might say I walked into a strange world. But they let me come home on Christmas."

Carl dropped out of Cortez High School and worked as a laborer, truck driver, cop and cowboy. He learned on the job from older Indian men and in 1981 was named head of natural resources. "I found out you never quit learning. This is what I made of myself with what little education I had. I learned a lot of things from those old guys." He spit in the corral and pointed a finger at his sternum. "This is not really me. It's me and everybody else that picked me up when I fell."

During the roundup, he talked quietly with buyers who gathered for a meal before the auction. Carl has hired white cowboys to manage most of the ranches and is loyal to his crew.

"I can handle men"—skills learned partly in the National Guard at Fort Carson. "That's when I found out what the outside world looks like. People there don't go day to day without having some kind of income. They've got to pay taxes, and they've got to pay for every little thing. Here [on the reservation] people can survive with what little they got," said Carl.

"The Indian way is kind of hard to understand. But then again, white men way is hard to understand, too."

In a room filled with Halloween orange, Gerrael and his pals began cutting pumpkins. "Stay on the line," the teacher said. "Good, Mary Jane, perfect. O.K. Gerrael, you did a good job." The kids put down their blunt scissors and began to draw at their tiny desks. "I have a family" was the assignment. They were to color faces for each person at home. Gerrael's crayon began with the hair. Soon, hair covered the paper. "That's a hairy person, isn't it?" the Indian teacher asked gently.

At Towaoc's Head Start, the children of the Ute Mountain Ute Reservation get a loving nudge toward school. Gerrael, who is three, will attend for three years before heading off to kindergarten in Cortez. It would seem a good beginning. "But something happens to those kids," said Judy Knight, Gerrael's grandmother. "They do fine here. When they get to Cortez, they say they don't behave. They stick them in special classes. They're immediately labeled because they're Indian."

Since 1961 children from the reservation have attended Cortez public schools. It has been a frustrating relationship, marked with distrust, disenfranchisement and too much failure. Despite the best intentions of both Utes and the school system, about half the Indian kids drop out before graduating from twelfth grade. It is estimated that only 30 percent of the adults in Towaoc finished high school. And while a number of bright students go on to college—twelve this year—only two tribal members have graduated from college. "It's obvious we haven't found the right answers," said school superintendent Roy Johnson.

According to interviews with Utes and school officials, the system falters for many reasons: English skills that are not up to school standards, standards that are culturally biased against Indians, apathy on the part of Indian parents, lack of role models and plain old prejudice—on both sides. "Each side is so suspicious, it's pathetic," said Johnson.

About 190 Ute students attend school in Cortez—7 percent of the student body—riding buses the fifteen miles each morning. On any given date, ten to forty kids are absent. The tribe employs a monitor who checks every absentee every day to keep the pressure on them. "You can have the best schools and the best teachers, but the student has to be there," said Sarah Wells, who directs the monitoring.

Even Gerrael has balked at getting up for Head Start. He often makes excuses not to go. But he doesn't have a choice. "I played hooky once in junior high," said Judy. "My mother reported me to tribal police. I spent a night in jail for skipping school." Judy drops Gerrael off at 8:00 A.M. and picks him up at 4:00 P.M. after a half-day of learning and a half-day of day care. As they walk down the steps of tribal headquarters, Judy makes him count "One, two ... ," he smacks his feet, "nine, ten. Good!"

Most reservation children are not exposed to enough books, outside cultures or problem-solving expected by schools, said Head Start chief Lorna Greene. Nor is their self-esteem very high, because of poverty. Boosting it is a key goal of Head Start.

One of the biggest problems is English. For although kids like Gerrael watch lots of TV and speak English instead of Ute, they learn it in households where it is mixed with Ute and nonverbal communications like sign language and "lip pointing." In an English-only system, that puts them behind classmates from the start.

At school, bilingual and remedial reading classes attempt to raise their skills, but that help—it usually means pulling the kid from his regular classroom—tends to label the child a slow learner, a stigma that defeats the very purpose of the help. "You're already marked, and the other kids know it," said Judy. "Does that mean you're dumb? Gerrael knows what an elephant is. He knows what an escalator is."

Despite the special help, test scores show that in the first six grades in Cortez, Indians fall further behind at the rate of one month per year. By the time they are in sixth grade, the Anglos score a grade level of 6.3 and the Indians 5.4, nine months back.

Cultural differences also are staggering for an Indian child. He goes from a world surrounded by familiar brown faces to one in which there are maybe two or three Indian faces in a classroom. He may come from a home without a telephone or a street address. And the school day is regimented by time, the work answer-oriented rather than thematic. "Everything we do is pretty contrary to what they're used to," said Gene Sparks, principal at Kemper Elementary. The kids also reflect, and suffer from, the attitudes of their communities. The schools play out the old cowboy-and-Indian mentality.

"Going into the fifth grade, I'd put on a new shirt and come home with it ripped, a blue eye and a fat lip—at least once a week," said Terry Knight. "They didn't know what we were, and we didn't like them either. A lot of times we initiated it."

Judy's son, Alvin, played sports with white kids, so felt part of the school. But four of his cousins, Gladys's children, felt pushed out of sports. Her three oldest children went to Indian boarding schools in Phoenix so they could play more.

This year, about forty Ute students attend Indian boarding schools. Three of them are daughters of Arthur Cuthair, a councilman-elect, who pulled them from Cortez schools after they were accused—unfairly, he says—of vandalism. "They're straight 'A' students now. The oldest plays basketball and led them to second place in state. She couldn't accomplish that here in Colorado."

Cuthair ran for the Cortez school board last year but lost in district-wide voting to a white man. He later filed suit in federal court, claiming discrimination and seeking an Indian district.

The Cortez school board agrees that an Indian on the board would help relations and may agree to a special district vote ensuring one. The board's attitude is part of a recent, and welcomed, thaw in relations between the school system and the reservation.

The board is less enthusiastic about a Ute proposal to operate a school for grades one to three on the reservation—"just like every other small community," said Judy. Board President Walt Henes worries that it might just "prolong the cultural shock." But both sides agree that the single most important ingredient has nothing to do with the board. Success starts with parents.

It was pushing from Kate Knight that got Judy through school. Terry, arrested after graduation for an alcohol violation, was bailed out by his grandmother with the news, "You're going to college."

"We had to go to school," said Judy. "You didn't answer back." As she talked, Gerrael approached with a book.

"Read this, Grandma."

She began leafing through Charlie Brown's *Cyclopedia.* "Do smart people have bigger brains?" "Why do people have different color skin?"

She was reading the questions. He squirmed away before she could read the answers.

12

Halloween Goblins and the Skinwalker

The menu at the Indian corner of Mesa Verde has a distinctly native flavor: Indian tacos and frybread—with or without hot dogs. Becky Hammond, who works there, loves to stand behind a line of hungry tourists queued up at the refreshment stand and shout, "Give me a Ute dog. And leave the tail on."

It's an inside joke—about eating dogs—and it invariably draws weird looks. Becky is used to being stared at and making jokes about it. She is a real, live Indian in a park dedicated to the remains of earlier inhabitants of the Four Corners. "There's one," some tourists say. "They point at me. They take video and say, 'Just stand there and talk.'"

Becky, Gladys's daughter, is a bright, fun woman of twenty-four in training at Santa Fe's Indian Institute of the Arts. This summer she worked at Soda Point, a tiny corner of Mesa Verde owned by the Ute Mountain Ute tribe. She sometimes pats dough into frybread at the refreshment stand. She also helps leasee Penny Livingston sell Indian-made souvenirs at a small shop set up on the Indian land just off the park's loop road, a road that carries thousands of tourists each year. "Penny wants me to wear a feather and get on a horse to stop traffic. She teases me."

But grabbing a bit more of the tourist trade is not a joking matter for the Ute Mountain Ute tribe. Mesa Verde belonged to the tribe before the United States carved out a national park in 1906—before anyone realized the economic potential of parks. Now 800,000 people visit year-round, and the tribe would like to sell more of them a Ute dog or jewelry or pots made by members. That would lead to more jobs and an opportunity to educate visitors about contemporary Indian culture.

When Mesa Verde National Park was created, officials built roads to the spectacular ruins on Chapin Mesa. The road crossed one tip of the mesa called Soda Point. Years later, surveyors discovered that the road slipped onto Indian land. The park moved the road in the 1960s but then found in another survey that about 300 yards of road still was on Ute land.

In 1986, the Utes took advantage of the mistake, setting up a souvenir-refreshment stand and helicopter rides along the road. The park objected to the looks of the stand, the traffic jams it created and the competition with its own concessionaire. It began to move the road again to cut the Utes off. But cooler heads prevailed, and the two sides have begun a two-year study of ways to develop Soda Point and divert some visitors to the tribal Anasazi ruins that surround Mesa Verde; the tribe has established its own primitive park on 125,000 acres. The study dovetails with a growing interest in Anasazi ruins. Congress is studying a national monument of Anasazi sites in the Four Corners area.

Becky knows firsthand the fascination of tourists, particularly foreigners, with Indians. As she worked to repair a beaded bracelet designed by her grandmother,

Kate, someone tried to buy it. She said another Ute artist working there was asked for his moccasins by a French visitor.

"Are you an Indian?" tourists ask her.

"No," says Becky, pointing to blonde-haired Penny. "But she is."

Becky is an athlete, a former shot putter, a softball player and mountain biker and a woman who appears comfortable with non-Indians and their naive attitudes. She chides them gently with flawless speech that jars them into the twentieth century. "People are always interested in how much education I have gotten. They'll say, 'You speak very good English for an Indian.'"

There also is a common perception that the Utes descended from the diminutive Anasazi who lived in a small-roomed cliff houses, abandoned about A.D. 1200. A visitor at Soda Point once asked Becky's uncle, Terry, this question, "What happened to you guys?"

"We got taller," said Terry.

Archaeologists say there is no cultural connection between the Anasazi, the "ancient ones," and the Utes. The Anasazi were farmers, raising crops atop Mesa Verde. Only in the last 100 years of their millennium stay did they build their cliff dwellings; then they moved south. The Anasazi were the ancestors of today's Pueblo Indians, including the Hopi and Zuni tribes.

The Utes came later, hunter-gatherers who grazed the valley of the Mancos River, which drains Mesa Verde and cuts its deep channels. They avoided the ruins and did not raid them for pots and bones. "When you disturb the spirits of the dead, then you die, too," they told a pioneering family that collected relics.

Asa House, the great grandfather of tribal chairman Ernest House, first took white men to the ruins in the 1870s, a move that led to the establishment of the national park. In the adjacent tribal park, the ruins have been left pretty much as they were found, whereas the national park has reconstructed and stabilized many on its side of the boundary. Instead of paved roads, the Indian park has dirt roads and rough trails. About 1,000 visitors visit each year. Soda Point, by contrast, may get fifty times that many, making it a highly visible outlet for beaders, painters and potters on the reservation.

Becky began making jewelry in high school and studied silversmithing in Santa Fe. When she returns in January, she hopes to take classes in museum curating, with an eye to working in a gallery. "I don't really plan on staying in Towaoc. The problem is jobs. There's not much to do."

The tribal study of Soda Point and its own park envisions a range of possibilities, from a motel at Soda Point to a tram up the mesa. Such development could keep tribal members like Becky on the reservation while educating tourists. They'll continue to be amazed at seeing a young Indian woman patting dough into frybread, wearing a T-shirt reading, "Saks Fifth Avenue."

"What?" they'll ask Becky Hammond, "are you doing with a shirt like that, way out here?"

As the canvas door closed, plunging us into darkness, the rocks in the pit glowed with life. I could feel it, see it— a dry, red heat that made me sweat.

When Terry Knight splashed water on the rocks, my body cried. I cried. Nearly naked in the night, I was face to face with something fundamental: earth, fire, water and air, in a tiny sweat lodge of chokecherry limbs. In their searing union I felt exposed, with nowhere to go but inside.

Terry had asked me to join his sweat, with two other members of the tribe. He wanted me to know something of his spiritual path, one that has led him to be regarded as "medicine man" on the reservation. He is called on often to help his people, to cure them of some dysfunction, be it physical or spiritual. The Utes do not see them as separate. Religion and medicine are one in traditional thinking. Their common enemy is evil, sickness, imbalance.

To walk the red path is to be healthy in mind, body and spirit. The sweat lodge is one of the tools. "It's not like a church where somebody reads from a book," said Terry. "It's spiritual enlightenment, purification, rejuvenation, from a person's own experience."

The sweat began as the sun flared down behind the toe of Ute Mountain, across the valley from Terry's house. In a nearby dry wash, thirty-five volcanic rocks sat in a wood fire. The sweat lodge was shaped like a dome tent with canvas and blankets on the wood frame. No metal is used in its construction. Inside, a pit was dug in the center. We sat cross-legged around it, on a narrow ledge, as the hot rocks were dropped into the pit, one by one. The number of rocks can vary according to the needs of the participants. The minimum is twenty-four. A forty-nine rock ceremony can raise blisters on the skin. Eighty rocks is called a power sweat.

When the door flap closed, Terry led prayers in a low, deep voice. Then he sang and dropped water on the rocks. We sweated profusely. It was an emotional time, too, high-temperature meditation, a feeling of being in touch with something elemental, within and without. The lodge is called by some the core of the universe. Others see a womb. When we took a break and went outside, the stars had wrapped us in a galactic blanket, shaped like the lodge itself.

"It brings us down to earth, to the basics of life," said Terry. "And that's the place to communicate with the Creator."

It is direct communication with God that makes Terry a medicine man. He claims no power himself. The healing is God's work. "I'm just a channel. I didn't ask for this gift. Those of us who have been blessed don't like to brag." He is reluctant to discuss the cures, or even call himself a medicine man. All he will say is that patients tell him he has helped end serious illnesses. But there are things he can't do, powers lost with the last legendary Ute medicine men.

When Terry was six, he saw Walter Lopez cure his mother, Kate, of gallstones. In a ceremony Lopez placed his head against her abdomen and spit the stones from his mouth into his hand. The man who removed stones from her in September—a white surgeon—doesn't believe such stories. In one recent gall bladder case he saw, a Navajo medicine man allegedly sucked the gallstones through the abdomen. But, "They looked like Dolores River rocks," said Dr. Gerald Howe.

Fraudulent medicine men exist, said Terry, acknowledging that he could not perform such a ceremony successfully. He prayed for Kate during the Sun Dance in July, but it was not enough. She then consulted Navajo medicine men several times before agreeing to surgery because of her acute condition and the difficulty of finding a trustworthy Indian healer.

With the traditional Ute healers dead, Utes who want to consult medicine men must call on Navajo medicine men in neighboring Arizona. They have their own association, specialties and rate charts that can range from $75 to several hundred dollars, said Dr. Karl Hansen, Kate's internist, who worked three years at the Towaoc Indian Health Service. In Cortez, he said, families often call a medicine man to the hospital. But he believes their power is confined to psychosomatic disorders—anxiety attacks, for example.

"A lot of diseases are intermittent. I personally don't believe that traditional Indian men can affect physiological disease processes. But that's my belief set. I wouldn't presume to tell someone else what they should believe."

I am prepared to believe in medicine men. There is wisdom in folk medicine that we are only beginning to understand. There are herbs that have scientific basis. Mormon tea, for example, a plant that grows on the Ute reservation and is brewed by Utes for colds, contains ephedrine, a decongestant and bronchial dilator. Sudafed, the commercial cold medicine, is pseudo or synthetic ephedrine.

But beyond herbs, I believe that there are forces and lessons in the natural world—miracles, perhaps—that we can't hear in the noise of civilization. Traditional medicine men led spartan, simple lives, close to the earth. Walter Lopez lived in a hogan and wore moccasins. He would not hunt with bullets. He could not think negative thoughts, tell lies or stand noise.

"The man, the power and the spirit were one," said Terry. "And that doesn't exist anymore. It would be hard to keep pure. There's too much greed. The temptations are too great." The tragedy is that the wisdom and power of these men are gone. "I have no one to learn from," he said.

Sweats and such practices as the peyote sacrament of the Native American Church are used to substitute for the medicine man. The collective power of people around the tent results in prayers being answered. On a full moon night, Terry invited me into a teepee to participate in a Native American Church ceremony. It began at sunset and lasted all night. Terry led the singing while shaking a gourd rattle and holding a staff. A drummer knelt by him, beating an iron drum filled with water and charcoal and covered with hide. Then he passed the staff and gourd to the next in the circle.

Ground-up peyote was passed in a plastic bucket, followed by peyote tea. But getting high was not the object. Like the sweat ceremony, the peyote helps move the worshippers to another plane of consciousness. "It puts you in a certain state of mind," said Terry, who has attended since childhood. His father, Charles, introduced the peyote ceremony to many Navajos in the 1920s. Elements of the ceremony are the same as a sweat: a fire in the middle, the womb of the tent, ashes spread on an altar of earth. At midnight and dawn a woman brings water to drink.

Carl Knight, Terry's brother, was the fire tender. "It can be used for whatever problem you've got," said Carl. "I eat that medicine, I think about and ask the Creator, 'Show me the way.' And every time, I find a way."

Bull Durham tobacco was smoked by those with special prayers. Emotions ran high. Men sobbed. "They feel the closeness to the spirit," said Terry. "They get one on one, and they know they will be heard and taken care of."

The goblins of Head Start fanned out across tribal grounds, shouting a familiar threat. "Trick or treat," they said at each door, their sacks gaping for goodies. Judy Knight's office was ready for them. Cobwebs hung from the ceiling and clock. Spiders glowed in the dark. As they filed through, the kids held hands and tried not to trip in their masks of ghoulish grins.

Halloween is a big time for the kids of Ute Mountain. At the recreation hall, the tribe held a Halloween party for the children with games and a dance. They bobbed for apples, held cake walks, shot baskets for prizes and got painted by older kids with spray cans. All-white ghost faces were popular.

George probably appreciated the company. He normally haunts the building alone. George is the name given to the spirit that has lived in the rec hall since a child drowned there. Becky Hammond heard George one night, springing off the diving board and splashing in the water. When she looked in the pool, it was empty. During remodeling he rummaged through lunch pails of the construction crew. "We've always known about George," said Reuben, Becky's twin brother.

The presence of spirits is accepted as fact by members of the Knight clan. It's a belief rooted in tradition and actual experience. Brenda Hammond hears ghosts all the time in the police station where she works. "Go away," she tells them. "I'm not scared of you." Gladys hears doors closing in her house. "Maybe it's my son" [who committed suicide], she said. "We were taught not to fear them," said Judy. "When they come around, we speak to them and ask what they want."

Like most Ute parents the Knights used ghost stories to get their kids inside and into bed at night. The "basket lady" is a common parental tool—she lives on Ute Mountain and eats little kids who stay out after dark. But there are good spooks and bad ones, daylight and dark, the devil and Creator, the two sides of life. The same medicine that could pull gallstones from Kate Knight could pull a man's heart out and make him die, said Terry. "You could do that if you have medicine of that caliber."

Terry speaks often of the devil on his tail, waiting for him to slip on his spiritual path. "You have to pay a price for the [healing] gift. It's a matter of people's lives—and your own."

Of all the spirits, the skinwalker is most troubling to the Utes. Malevolent, speedy, he is able to hide in the skin of black dogs—or people. The skinwalker visits those who've been witched. "They do exist," said Terry. "It's the Indian version of the demon." A long time ago, skinwalkers were revered warriors of the Navajo, able to transform themselves into coyotes or foxes and go among their enemy for reconnaissance. When the Indian wars stopped, their power was used for evil. "In order to be a skinwalker you have to kill one of your kin. They can take your soul."

Judy and Becky both have heard skinwalkers and both describe the sound as a heavy horse galloping at night, breathing hard. One dashed past Judy's house at dawn. Becky heard one while jogging. Terry claims to have seen them: a large black dog with red eyes. "It leaves no tracks and can move like the wind. I've shot at them at night. If you see them it's a real bad taboo. So people come to me and ask me to fan them off [with an eagle wing], burn cedar and pray."

Last June near Towaoc, Terry used those tools to exorcise an evil spirit from a nephew in a case so bizarre it defies belief. But after separate interviews with Terry, Judy and the nephew, there is no doubt something happened.

Charlie Lehi, twenty-two, a young man raised by Judy, was walking home near Towaoc about 1:00 A.M. when he crossed a bridge over Navajo Wash. "I saw things standing on the bridge," he said. "It came behind me. It was like a line, a shadow. All of a sudden it jumped on my back. I started hazing out. I just kept praying. I yelled God's name. I thought it went away."

Two months later, in June, while walking near Judy's house, Charlie collapsed, paralyzed. Friends hauled him to Judy's, where he began convulsing. "You could hear something speaking out of Charlie," recalled Judy. "It was like the movie *Exorcist*, but things weren't flying around. This thing was laughing. It was unbelievable."

While four people held Charlie to the floor, Terry called for an eagle's wing, a bone whistle and a fire to burn cedar. "It had a deep husky voice and was saying, 'You can't get me.' It was spooky," said Terry.

The first whistle was broken. When he blew, it made no sound. "This thing laughed and said, 'It won't work,'" said Judy, who scrambled to find another whistle.

Terry straddled the young man and began fanning him with the wing, praying. "I could see that demon in my mind. It was either the demon or me. I told him I'm a living person of the Creator."

When the fire started and Terry began to burn cedar seeds, the husky voice erupted from Charlie: "No, no. Don't burn it, don't burn it." In an hour of wrestling with the young man, Terry chased the demon out. "It scared the hell out of me."

For days after, Judy's dogs barked. "We'd look and there was nobody there. It was not a skinwalker. It was more like a ghost," she said. She paused in her story. "It's not only Indian people who have ghosts. That's why you have church. To chase the devil. There's always the good and the bad."

As for Charlie, now working as a cook in the tribal headquarters, he apparently got the message. "Now," he said, "I go to church twice on Sundays and once on Wednesdays."

The Sleeping Ute received its first, light blanket of snow the other day. The dawn smelled like frost, and sunset like burning leaves. Carl Knight came home from the high country with cattle for the winter. Terry Knight watched his boy Conan play high school football and win. And outside the Hammonds', Becky piled firewood, brother Nick skinned a deer, and Gladys, their mother, cooked meat on a camp grill, sitting close to chase the chill. What white men call Indian summer had arrived on the reservation.

In two months, I have learned a bit of the rhythms of this place and the movements of one family. I pretty much know where to find them or where to wait. I'm comfortable now with being the odd man out, a feeling that comes not from treatment by the Knights but from something inside: the knowledge that I'm the minority here, and a snooping one at that.

Halfway through this series on Indian life, it is remarkable how much I've learned—and how little I know. It's apparent that readers have the same reaction. A few people have called me to thank me for the newspaper stories. Nearly all say it's important to learn about Indians. While in Gunnison recently, several people asked whether Charlie had found his goats. He has not and assumes someone stole them off Ute Mountain. But there is not the visceral response like that felt for the Spann Ranch stories written in spring. The reality of reservation life is sobering. And for most readers there is no common background with this indigenous tribe. No white dreams of growing up to be an Indian. Even some Indians are reluctant to do that.

Ute reaction, on the other hand, has ranged from cool indifference to shy pride at having their pictures and words in the paper. When I first arrived on the reservation, there was plenty of suspicion. The Ute Mountain tribe has had its share of being studied. One book ten years ago painted a vicious, demoralizing picture. It recounted the troubled 1960s when the FBI investigated claims of missing millions in tribal funds. There was plenty of outside press about that. And here I came, another hairy man from the East.

"What good will it do?" challenged Carl when we met. For a long time he kept himself at arm's length. "I like to poke strange things with a long stick," he said.

Charlie, his father, assumed we were selling his picture, taking without leaving anything—until I climbed to the top of 9,800-foot Ute Mountain to look for the goats. Gladys and her children invited me to supper on my first visit, and they probably have noticed since that I show up regularly, suspiciously close to mealtime. They, too, asked tough questions about my role.

There is no tradition of journalism on the reservation, not even for common reports like the tribal budget. But there is hunger for news. My stories are pinned to bulletin boards and read to adult education classes. The students complain that the Knights get all the attention but find "it comforting to know that other people know they exist," said GED teacher Jim Jindra.

When I wrote about Judy Knight's political views, it was such a revelation that an opponent photocopied it for his campaign literature. Judy, who will be inaugurated as tribal chairman on Friday, saw the series as a way of balancing the image outsiders have of her reservation. "When I got on council [in 1979], everything I heard about the tribe was negative," she said. "We were forgotten. People in Colorado don't know there are two Ute tribes." She also wants her people to "know where they've come from and be proud of themselves."

Terry hopes the articles will help him teach old traditions to a new generation. "Show me what you showed the white man reporter," he wants them to say. "I will—and more."

Already the series has prompted some letters to Judy offering business deals. One woman wanted to run busloads of tourists to the reservation. When Judy offered to run it by the council, the woman said she couldn't wait that long.

I also have received a call from an office at the University of Colorado asking my views on the tribe's needs. My answer will be simple: go to the reservation and talk to the people. It is uncomfortable to go to a foreign land— particularly one in our midst, one that we have ignored for so long. But continuing reluctance pays a price—misunderstanding, bias and bigotry.

There are times when I think that whatever footprints I've made here will soon be covered by drifting snows on Ute Mountain. Then I think of Ute perseverance, and think that some impression, however slight, will remain.

13

Sovereignty and the Autumn Taste of Jerky

*G*ladys Knight Hammond emerged from the basement in her sweats, fresh from a bout with the "Body Blaster." With the back of her hand, she wiped her brow and brushed back a clump of long black hair streaked the color of steel. Sweating from the workout, she slumped in a chair by the TV, exhaled hard, and spoke her mind. "Diet? That's a white man's word. Who wants to eat rabbit food all the time?"

She was mostly joking. Gladys is committed to exercise and weight loss—to save her life. A year ago she was diagnosed with diabetes. This fall she went on a liquid diet, losing twenty-six pounds in ten weeks. She wants to lose fifty more, to 150. "I can't have any fried stuff or fat meats. No sugar. I go on and off, I admit it. But I work at the health clinic and I see all these people come in with diabetes, and they don't take care of themselves. They start with pills and then shots, and eventually they're on dialysis machines."

On the reservation, obesity is widespread. There are also high rates of adult diabetes, arteriosclerosis, hypertension, strokes, blindness and gall bladder disease, all associated with obesity. In a culture where bread fried in lard is as common as hamburger, that may not be surprising. But Indian Health Service doctors are beginning to suspect genetics and life-style, as much as diet, as culprits.

"Indians used to survive feast and famine cycles. They had to put on weight in the summer for the winter," said Karl Hansen, the former IHS physician in Towaoc and Gladys's private doctor. "In my mind, there is no doubt that Utes are genetically predisposed to obesity. They don't consume any larger quantities of food than the rest of us. They're just more efficient at metabolism. They can really put weight on in a hurry."

Fifty years ago, when Gladys was a toddler, Utes lived a rugged, outdoor existence. Deer meat was a staple; her grandmother dried fruit for the sweet tooth. Salads were not part of their diet. Later, on the reservation, they began getting government commodities, carbohydrates mostly, and high-fat, high-salt foods.

Gladys still keeps a balance at home—fruit, salads, good meat grilled. She rarely buys cookies, and potato chips never. But her physical activity, like most Utes today, is minimal: swinging grandchildren, patting tortillas, filing papers at the IHS clinic. The American habit of three meals a day simply overloads her system.

A gentle soul who screams her heart out at Bronco games, Gladys was convinced by Dr. Hansen that with weight loss and exercise she could beat diabetes. So she began spending time in the storeroom downstairs. There her children set up a rowing machine, a bicycle and a weight bench. The kids are athletic, but nearly all face the same weighted future—compounded by the modern temptations of fast junk food.

The tribe has begun an aerobics program, a walking club and nutrition counseling. Barbie Johnson, the fitness coordinator, says many of her clients are 5-foot-2 women weighing 250 pounds. "They realize they're all too heavy. But weight loss is not my object now. The object is to get them involved, to improve their self-esteem. Exercise breeds positive self-image."

Health fairs have shown that despite obesity, cholesterol levels in Utes are within healthy ranges. But because of their metabolism, the Utes may have to work twice as hard to lose the same weight.

Gladys said nutrition information is beginning to have an impact. The IHS clinic talks about it more, and older women of her generation are just beginning to understand the connection between weight and diabetes. "I guess before it didn't soak in." When her children were young, Gladys cooked with little thought to nutrition. The Utes have no comparable word in their language. Today the kids do most of the cooking, and mealtime is a warm family event. Saturday morning they fill a big table at a Cortez restaurant; Sunday morning it's pancakes at home. And Sunday night is cookout time: outdoors by the brush arbor until the snow flies, then inside on the hearth.

Except for homemade tortillas, jerky and an occasional Navajo dish of grilled sheep intestine filled with fat, their fare looks like any well-fed American family's: bacon and eggs, cereal, potatoes, squash, beans, cornbread and hamburgers. And, oh yes, Pizza Hut pickups.

From now until Thanksgiving, though, those foods will only tempt Gladys. She's sticking to a thermos of chocolate-flavored Medifast. If Oprah Winfrey can do it, she reasons, so can she.

Behind Carl Knight's house, the blood-dark strips hung in the wind and dried. Pungent odors of wild game swirled through the cottonwood shade house. Carl's dogs walked beneath the meat, sniffing. "The foods that I grew up with are different: rabbits, deer, berries and roots, things of that sort," said Carl. "Now, rather than going to the store twelve months of the year, I go out and get a deer and fix it."

Carl's wife, Leora, peels the meat from the carcass, hangs it outdoors, then turns the strips each day for even drying. The process takes about two weeks. "We dry it and hang it up in a good bag." To tenderize it before eating, they "pound the heck out of it."

Jerking meat is as traditional as an activity gets on the Ute Mountain reservation. Despite refrigeration and supermarkets, jerky remains an important gastronomical—and cultural—artifact. Ute families eat it perhaps once a week during winter. The dried meat is mixed with corn in stew, ground and fried in lard or eaten as is, like a snack. Elk meat is jerked too, but better cuts of elk are frozen as steaks.

"I'm not just out there shooting animals for the fun of it," said Carl. "Hunting is a way of life for the Indian." The Utes still use their old hunting grounds for most of their big game—nearly 6,000 square miles of the San Juan Mountains. The land was bargained away from the Utes in 1873 to allow mining. But the United States agreed in exchange to let the Utes hunt there "so long as the game lasts and the Indians are at peace with the white people." That agreement was largely forgotten for more than a century by everyone but the Utes—until 1976, when an Indian hunter got stopped bringing home a buck. He was charged by state wildlife officials with hunting without a state license.

That's when Colorado and thousands of white residents learned that Congress had agreed to let Ute hunters roam from Cortez to Pagosa Springs and from Ridgway to Lake City. They had been doing it for decades without state licenses. "It was like every other treaty," said Carl. "It was said, written and just left lying there. When they discovered it, there was a lot of hot water."

After the Utes filed a federal lawsuit against the state in 1978, seeking continuation of their rights, many white residents of Montezuma County opposed what they considered special hunting privileges for Indians. State hunting seasons are restricted to a few weeks in the fall. In a negotiated settlement, the Weeminuche hung onto their hunting grounds, the "Brunot agreement area," named for the Indian agent who negotiated it in 1873. As a result they are allowed to hunt virtually anytime, without a state license, for "subsistence, religious or ceremonial purposes."

Opponents did insist on language that keeps Indian hunters away from towns, roads and parks. "They were afraid Indians were going to shoot up the countryside," said Dick Fentzlaff, the district wildlife manager. Ute hunters need only follow tribal game regulations—which parallel the state's—and carry tribal permits. They are handed out by a tribal commission, which Carl Knight chairs. "I can go to the commission and ask for a permit in January if I run out of food," said Carl.

In practice, most Indian hunting is done in the fall between early August and late November, before, during and after the state seasons. "That's a lot of hunting time, and many whites are envious," said Fentzlaff. "They're still against the idea, but not as hot under the collar about it."

About 300 Utes hunt regularly, and their impact is not significant. They represent less than 2 percent of the hunters in the area, and their success ratio is only 5 or 10 percent better than non-Indians who hunt the same area with state licenses, said Fentzlaff. The Brunot area remains well managed for game, unlike the Ute Mountain Ute Reservation, where the deer population has declined drastically. "The hunting on the reservation is the worst it's ever been," said Terry Knight, also a commission member. He blames constant hunting, in part stemming from increased poverty. "There's almost no regulation of hunting on the reservation. The hunting pressure is very high. The habitat is not what it used to be. We'll have to have a hunting code."

But proposed regulations to manage the game have been held up by a tribal council reluctant to restrict a tradition. Hunting was once the mark of manhood in Ute families. A boy grew up when he could provide meat.

Ute women today still refrain from eating deer meat while menstruating; it spoils their man's future hunts.

Deer antlers and meat also are used in ceremonies in the Native American Church. And a few old-timers still tan buckskin, using the leg bone to scrape the hair and the brain to soften the leather. The Utes once were renowned for their tanning.

But most Utes still hunt for the usual reasons: food, getting away or the late autumn taste of jerky. "I get tired of that store food," said Carl. "Something inside tells me, enough. So I go out and get a deer."

The pickup truck rolled out of Towaoc into a Sunday morning sun. The truck's bed rattled with poles and barbed wire, and the cab reverberated with the sound of drum songs coming from the radio. Judy Knight leaned to turn up the Indian program and giggled at something said in Ute. Her face was softer in the warm light; her mood improved. The divisive election and inauguration were behind her. The chairman of the Ute Mountain Ute tribe was getting away for a day—to fix fence.

"I didn't think the queen had to fix fence," I said, and she giggled again.

"Yep," said Bob Frank, her husband at the wheel. "When her old man calls, even the queen has to work."

He turned south at the bingo hall and drove toward New Mexico. The sun rose past Chimney Rock and Mancos Canyon. The talus was deeply shadowed. The country opened up as we crossed the river. Utah lay west twenty dry miles and the Navajo nation ahead, beyond the peak called Shiprock. To the east, some miles away, grazed the Knight cattle on a portion of the reservation in New Mexico. Judy's father had found a couple of gaps in a fence. "Those cattle could get out, and then the Navajo will put their brands on them," she said.

Calling Judy "queen" was only half in jest, because she is, in many respects, a sovereign. She heads a sovereign government, and the land we were driving through is a sovereign nation. "I will exercise the right of self-government," Judy had sworn in taking office two days before.

Sovereign status is rooted in the nation-to-nation treaties signed with Xs by tribal leaders when the United States needed their peace in the nineteenth century. Early Supreme Court cases defined their place as "domestic dependent nations," subject only to the government that conquered them. After 150 years of legal and political struggle, that precedent is even more deeply implanted. "This tribe has jurisdiction over its land, its members and anyone on the reservation doing business here," said Judy Leaming, the tribal attorney. "Tribal sovereignty is unique. It is absolute."

Bob turned off the highway and began a rutted ride into the backcountry. Judy grew up here in a hogan. Her father rode the fenceline for the tribe. "Turn here," Judy said to Bob. She touched his hand and pointed from memory. "The fence is broken over by the big smoke." That's what her father called the San Juan power plant. Around us, old pumpjacks sucked Ute oil, a good example of Ute sovereignty. The tribe has levied taxes against oil and gas companies since the 1920s.

Legally, sovereignty means the tribe can run its own government under its own constitution. It includes a chief executive, a council and a tribal court that handles adoptions, civil and criminal cases. If a Cortez merchant is owed money by a Ute, for example, he can go into tribal court for payment. Speeders can be handled in tribal court, too. For the most part, the tribe has equal status with the state of Colorado. It claims sovereign immunity against suit, like one filed in county court this year for payment of a debt by a tribal councilman. The court threw it out. Moreover, the state cannot levy an income tax on tribal members who work on the reservation. Neither can the state regulate the tribe's bingo operation, which hands out thousands of dollars in prizes on weekends.

But recently the state of New Mexico won a Supreme Court decision allowing a state tax on oil pumped from reservations in New Mexico. That oil already is taxed by the Utes, making its oil more expensive. The decision is considered a setback in Indian country because it directly attacks a tribe's ability to support itself, the key to economic self-determination.

Bob stopped the pickup near the "big smoke" and found the fence hole, a fifteen-foot section broken by a flash flood in the gully. The old wire was intact, tangled in mud and tumbleweed. We dug it out, pounded new posts and patched the hole. "The other hole is where the man with the gold teeth lives," said Judy, pointing the way. "That's what we call him."

The pickup ground out of the soft arroyo and out onto a mesa where outcrops of coal showed in seams. Someday the strip mine by the power plant could extend onto Ute land.

The unique aspect of tribal sovereignty is that Judy's tribe remains a ward of the federal government. The land is held by the United States in trust for the tribe. The Bureau of Indian Affairs superintendent signs off on the tribal budget and the council's major decisions. In turn, Uncle Sam's agents are expected to safeguard such things as the tribe's oil and gas rights, something they failed to do in the New Mexico oil district. Because of an error in surveying, oil wells thought to be on the Ute reservation actually were on

Navajo land. Judy's tribe lost $7 million in royalties to the Navajos. "It's back to the good old U.S. government," she said. "The survey was off, and we're stuck with the problems the government created for us."

Bob stopped the pickup and we stepped out, trying to find the break. The sun had moved west, and the air was warm. We walked a fenceline to the edge of a wash, scanned the horizon with binoculars but couldn't find the break. We ate lunch on the tailgate. Boiled meat and potatoes. It was quiet except for the squawk of a pumpjack.

"Can you imagine being out here at night and hearing that?" said Bob. A coyote loped by and Bob offered his rifle. I declined. "My father always said if you kill a coyote, you'll start to act like him," he said.

The Ute Mountain Utes increasingly equate sovereignty with knowledge. Judy has learned how to read royalty contracts and has set up a tribal energy office with an accountant and an inspector. They do jobs once handled by guardian Uncle Sam. The tribe also hired its own water experts and lawyers to negotiate its ancient water rights. Tribal attorney Leaming says sovereignty issues are a "never ending battle. We are always fighting for acknowledgment of sovereignty."

We headed back the long way, over a mesa still inhabited by Navajos in hogans. It was a route Judy used to travel as a girl, in the back of a wagon. As the truck rolled toward the edge, we could see Ute Mountain, Mesa Verde and much of Judy's reservation stretched out in the autumn, afternoon sun.

Like their Navajo neighbors, the Utes have an intact land, unbroken by private property that plagues other reservations. It is their greatest sovereign treasure.

Bob stopped the truck for a moment, to take in the view. A beautiful kingdom, I said to myself and looked at Judy. In the play of soft light on her face, I thought I could detect just a little pride. She was on top of the world.

The two men stood in a maze of tanks, talking quietly as a valve flapped. As the gas passed, it made a soft metallic click. One man held a wrench and watched a gauge. The other man watched him. Behind them an oil well pumped up and down, eight strokes a minute, 100 barrels a day. Its engine, said the man with the wrench, ran on natural gas from the well and pumped oil to huge tanks that stood nearby. Excess gas went through the valve where he stood and then to a pipeline to be measured.

"This is the meter," said Gordon Hammond, the second man. "The oil goes to Four Corners Pipeline, then to refineries in Long Beach, California, or Bloomfield, New Mexico."

He pointed the way the oil flowed, away from Ute Mountain and the reservation where he lived. "Our goal is to make sure the tribe is getting what it's supposed to. That's where most of the money comes from."

Gordon, the thirty-year-old son of Gladys Knight Hammond, is the Ute Mountain Utes' oil field compliance officer. What he represents is growing tribal savvy in mineral matters. "All this was really new to me," said Gordon, a husky ex-Marine called "Bear" by his family. He joined the new tribal energy department in 1983 after a stint on a seismic crew. "I'm certified to conduct oil and gas inspections. I go through the lease files, production records. I go on location and check that they are complying with safety and environmental regulations." Gordon's work is part of the tribe's attempt to redress decades of mismanagement, if not outright theft, of oil and gas.

The oldest well on the reservation dates to 1921. In the 1950s, dozens more were drilled, pouring millions of dollars into the tribe's coffers. With that money the tribe paid for all its services—police and medical and welfare. With the decline in the price of oil—from $32 per barrel in 1984 to $13 per barrel in 1988—the tribe's government has had to scale back, too. "We are on the downside," said Judy Knight, Gordon's aunt.

Had the tribe known what it does today, revenues would be higher. Like most tribes, the Utes relied on the Bureau of Indian Affairs to negotiate leases. Most of them were standard at 12.5 percent of gross revenues at a time when leases on private land were as high as 15 percent. Today, the tribe insists on 16 to 20 percent, plus bonuses. The early leases also were long-term, allowing the tribe no chance to renegotiate as market conditions changed. Some of the 1950s leases are still in effect.

The tribe also suspects that oil was stolen from dozens of wells in remote areas. Tanker trucks could drive to the well and open a valve. The BIA, charged with monitoring, rarely did. "The extent of loss was never computed," said Ahmed Kooros, chief economist with the Denver-based Council of Energy Resource Tribes (CERT) and an advisor to the Ute Mountain Utes.

Incredibly, until 1982 the Interior Department's position was that Indians could not develop their own mineral properties. They had to lease it to someone else. Since 1983 the tribe has hired an accountant and inspector Hammond to watchdog the oil wells. He's visited every well—more than 200. "Now the companies are aware that the tribe is watching," said Kooros.

CERT, which Judy chairs, was instrumental in restoring fairness in Indian energy matters. It taught tribes the tricks of the trade. It created new formulas to measure, for example, the value of open Indian land to energy companies that wanted to cross it. With Kooros's help the Ute Mountain Utes raised pipeline right-of-way fees from fifty cents per rod to $74 per rod, in some cases. In another instance, a road used to haul coal across the southeast corner of the reservation was leased for $815,000 plus tolls that will return $15 million to the tribe over time. When regarded strictly as a dirt road in grazing country it was worth only $3,200.

The tribe now is looking at inequities in electric rates. An ugly 340-kilovolt power line from New Mexico crosses the reservation in two places, carrying wholesale power at two cents a kilowatt-hour. The tribe receives nothing for the right-of-way and pays nearly nine cents a kilowatt-hour for its power from the local cooperative, said Kooros.

Unfortunately, this newfound sophistication comes near the end of the known oil and gas reserves on the reservation. Gordon's tribe has only another ten years of pumping before the existing wells go dry. So the tribe has begun to funnel 10 percent of its oil revenue to investments to create other kinds of jobs. It also has begun to tax the oil companies, revenues that now equal the amount from royalties. "Taxes and tribal enterprises are all we're going to have pretty soon," said Judy.

Studies show possible methane and carbon dioxide deposits beneath the reservation. And tremendous amounts of coal lie several hundred feet below. Getting to it, though, would create massive scars. Higher prices of oil also could spark exploration for deeper deposits. "There is oil there, but they say it's not economical to produce," said Gordon. "It's a nonrenewable resource we have—and it's in a decline now."

14

"We Shot
Our Arrows
at Them ... "

*T*he third-grade writing assignment began fairly simply: "The year is 1800. You and your family are traveling by covered wagon over the mountains to your new home in the West."

Oraleigh Hammond, eight, one of the five Indian students in the Cortez Elementary School class, glanced at the wagon pictured on the paper, and read on: "You keep a diary and write down your exciting experiences. You have bad weather, Indian trouble and many other problems. Write down what you see, feel and hear."

Ora, as she's called by her family on the Ute reservation, put a big X over "Indian" and began writing on the lines provided:

"It was almost sunset. We decided to explore the rest of our land. ... We heard something coming down the road. We got our arrows together."

While other students began telling tales of dead Indians, Ora, with her teacher's urging, stuck to her version of history: "We looked and there were seven cuberd [sic] wagons. We shot our arrows at them. We killed some. The seven wagons followed us. ... We shot more and more and more arrows. We got most of them."

But not all, as Ora no doubt knows. The whites in the wagons carved homesteads and towns from Indian country and stayed. Her own mother is white, married to Ruby Hammond, the vice-chairman of the tribe. Her grandmother, Gladys, is a Knight.

What is remarkable about the school assignment—aside from its insensitivity—is how it encapsulizes Cortez history from the white point of view. As Ora's effort shows, there are two versions. And the difference marks the starting point for relations between Cortez and the reservation, relations that only now are beginning to overcome the histories. "When I came here fifteen years ago, it was cowboys versus Indians," said Tim Wood, the sheriff of Montezuma County. "There were fights, antagonism. It was the Friday night knife and gun club."

Two years ago, in a ceremony marking a turnaround, the Cortez Chamber of Commerce named the Ute Mountain Ute tribal council its "Citizen of the Year." Still, relations remain sensitive because reservation border towns suffer the clash of cultures. "We try to get along with those people," said Judy Knight, the tribal chairman.

"The relationship is tolerance—I'd hesitate to say cordial," said Bob Helms, who owns the Toggery clothing store and presented the chamber award to the tribe. "There's definitely a gulf there."

Cortez was created in 1886 by land speculators selling irrigated farmland. The reservation's borders were not settled for another eight years, leading to the "Indian trouble."

Until the 1950s when oil royalties filled their pockets, Utes didn't go to Cortez much. They bartered at trading posts run by whites like Byron Pyle, still in business at the edge of the reservation. They sold cattle and crafts for credit. With their new cash, the Indians went to town, buying trucks, refrigerators, TVs and booze. Many Utes didn't know values and were ripped off. Both sides tell sad stories from that era. At the time, agriculture and mining were mainstays of the local economy. Both have declined.

Tourism now is considered the leading industry, although merchants have slowly realized the economic value of the reservation, which pours nearly $5 million into Cortez each year—half of it steady, federal dollars. The reservation has become the largest employer in the county. Little wonder that Cortez businesses began sponsoring a Native American Appreciation Day. "If the Utes ever decided they didn't want to do business, Cortez would dry up and blow away," said Randy Adair, whose family runs a bike shop and fried chicken outlet.

But that commerce is also the grist for friction between Utes and whites. Based on some bad experiences, merchants still harbor attitudes that Utes are lazy and not to be trusted. They say they cannot collect bad debts on the reservation.

The most talked about problem is drunk Indians, who this summer made a nuisance in the city park, next to a state tourism center. The drunks panhandled from tourists. Police estimate that only ten to fifty people are responsible for the public drinking, one-third of them Ute. They drink in town because it is illegal on the reservation. "Those guys give a black eye to the whole tribe," said Helms, a sentiment shared by the Hammonds. "They see an Indian in the park and think we're all drunks," said Brenda Hammond, Ora's aunt.

Most whites in Cortez also consider the Utes guarded and suspicious. Yet very few whites travel to Towaoc. They expect to be run off the reservation. They rarely get to know Utes at home, in work or worship settings. So the obligation for improved relations rests with the Utes who travel to town and in acts great and small leave an impression.

Oraleigh Hammond's work in school does that; so does her participation in dancing lessons or her purchases at McDonald's. The Hammonds go to town regularly, to shop or eat out. Gladys attends most school parent functions and has a reputation among principals for speaking her mind. She saw Ora's wagon story posted at a parents' night.

"Rather than being a secluded little colony, you start talking one on one and you realize there is an intelligence there," said Sheriff Wood. But it takes years to change attitudes and images. More than a century after the wagons came west, there are people in Cortez who resent the special status of the Ute Mountain Ute Reservation and consider it just welfare.

And there is still a little Ute girl who fantasizes this ending to her story: "There was only one family out of the wagon train left. One day one of our men said he saw somebody. Sure enough. There was the wagon. We killed them. The battle was over. We won!"

Alyssa liked her birthday cake so well she wore it—all over her pudgy face. Some chocolate icing may have reached her mouth, but she didn't seem to notice. It was, after all, the second cake of the day for her. She had turned the "big two," and her foster family at Gladys Knight Hammond's doted on her. There were two parties, a Little Minnie doll and lots of hugs.

In Alyssa's year at Gladys's there had never been a shortage of hugs. Or laps. Or love. It had been the best year of her life. Details of her first year are locked up in juvenile court, which last week accepted Alyssa's mother's aching decision to terminate her own parental rights. The decision came two weeks after Alyssa's birthday.

What is known is that Alyssa and her mother were

victims of alcohol and that the joy generated by the girl's presence in one household came only after the collapse of another. The young mother had once been a ward of the court herself because of her mother's alcohol abuse. She represented a vicious cycle all too common on the Ute Mountain Ute Reservation.

Here, 97 percent of social service cases are related to alcohol or drug abuse.

Here, 98 percent of cases before tribal court are alcohol or drug related.

Here, 80 percent of the population frequently uses drugs or alcohol to excess.

The effects reach into every corner of the reservation, from jobs to education. Life expectancy is thirty-eight years due to accidents or violence caused by drinking. Eighty-five percent of driving age members have lost their licenses because of alcohol. "There is not a single tribal member who is not adversely affected in one manner or another as a result of substance abuse," according to a tribal report.

Members of the Knight family have been touched like all the rest. Drinking is a painful subject to discuss, and no one throws stones very far. "I've tasted that stuff," said Carl. "I stopped drinking twenty years ago. But if you've been down that road, you can't refuse somebody help." "I've been on that road myself," said Terry. "I've been in alleys in Cortez. I've been in jail. I've begged and borrowed for a dollar to buy wine."

Alyssa came into their lives when Brenda, Gladys's thirty-one-year-old daughter and a police dispatcher, stopped at the tribe's youth shelter on business. Alyssa, then one year old and a ward of the court since the age of three months, walked up to her. "She wanted me to pick her up," said Brenda, who subsequently became the foster parent.

About seventy Ute children are in foster homes,

placements "primarily associated with alcohol abuse," said Melinda Bronson, director of social services for the tribe. Neglect is the primary problem—"children left alone, left in cars, left with inappropriate people."

Alyssa's mother said she never drank around Alyssa, but alcohol affected her judgment. Alyssa was abused once when left with an intoxicated relative, she said. The young woman had been a foster child until she turned eighteen, when she married a drinker. Within two years, her first child was in a foster home. Alyssa followed. She admitted that she did not keep up with a court-ordered plan of alcohol counseling and parenting classes. But she said she felt pushed by social services toward termination of her parental rights and did it "in the best interest of my children. I was a victim of alcohol, and Alyssa was, too, through me."

Until 1957, it was illegal to sell alcohol to Indians. It still is illegal to possess it on the reservation, but the fifty-odd cases of Budweiser in the tribal police evidence locker tell a different story. "There's lots of binge drinking," said police chief Mark Chagnon. Payday weekends are especially troublesome. "The reason people drink here are the reasons people drink to excess in other places."

But since the days when fur traders took advantage of Indians with fire water, there has been speculation that Indians are more susceptible to alcohol. And doctors who work with Indian alcoholism feel there is a genetic or metabolic predisposition, just as there is in 20 percent of the whole U.S. population. Studies are inconclusive. One Canadian study indicated that Indians absorb alcohol from the gastrointestinal tract faster, get high faster and sober up faster. But many Indians can drink socially without getting drunk.

"Most doctors speculate that a genetic predisposition is there, based on clinical and anecdotal evidence," said Dr. Craig Vandenwagen, director of clinical and preventive services for the Indian Health Service in Washington. He said the first good study won't be completed for another five years. If a genetic link is shown, Indian people could more readily accept alcoholism as a disease and stop linking it with moral failure. Doctors do not discount the strong "environmental" causes for excessive drinking: role models in families, low self-esteem, poverty and hopelessness.

"The wild, warrior spirit is still inside us," said Terry. "But assimilation is still going on. Young men seeking adventure can't live on the reservation with rules and regulations. So they go down the road. They say, 'I can't shine like that, so I'll shine in my dreams.' I tell them they'll die. And they say, 'I'm dying anyway.'"

Such a defeatist attitude is considered the biggest barrier to breaking the cycle. "It's almost socially accepted," said Tom Cole, who heads the tribe's employee assistance program. Getting Utes to admit that a problem exists is a key goal in a program of counseling, workshops and esteem-builders like a 100-mile walking club that the entire Hammond family—including Alyssa—is enrolled in.

If Utes live past forty, many dry out and abstain from alcohol. But the die is often cast for the next generation. The incidence of fetal alcohol syndrome, in which babies are born addicted, is the highest in the world—seven times the national average.

Alyssa was not a victim of that. Her mother said she didn't drink during her pregnancy. Like all kids, Alyssa likes her sweets but munches on apples after day care. She also plays with a puppy who nips at her shoes. Sometimes, when she's dressed in her purple sleepsuit, she'll sing "tinkle, tinkle little star" for "Daana," her best effort at pronouncing "Brenda."

This Christmas she may get a pedal car or a rocking horse. Early next year she may get a permanent home through adoption proceedings. The Hammonds are one family applying for her. "Alyssa is very dear to me and always will be," said her mother. "I just want her to be placed in a home where there is a lot of love and discipline."

For Alvin Pinnecoose, it's a long way from Ute Mountain, home of his tribe, to McNichols Arena, home of his Nuggets, the Denver professional basketball team. Choosing between them is like choosing a lover. They're both seductive. "I like the city. I like to go to Nuggets games. There are benefits here," he said from a cafe booth on Denver's Colfax Avenue. "The family is back home. It's cheaper on the reservation, and my friends are there. But once you've been to the city, it's tough to go back. The benefits aren't there. Towaoc is always going to be dead."

Alvin's dilemma is a microcosm of the tribe's. His choice of staying or leaving is one faced by nearly every youngster on the Ute Mountain Ute Reservation. The choice usually centers on jobs, but it also involves family, culture and life-styles.

The dilemma faces every parent, too. "Alvin should go out and do what he can," said Alvin's mother, Judy Knight. "He's got his own life to live. Maybe Alvin will come back someday." As tribal chairman, Judy is trying to create jobs to keep people home, reduce the brain drain and create a work ethic that was lost for many Utes after they were confined to the reservation.

Alvin, twenty-four, was named after his father, Judy's first husband. Alvin is a dark-haired introspective man with a quick smile. He is enrolled in a Lakewood construction school, learning skills to be a master carpenter. A tribal construction company is paying his tuition, hoping he'll return. But Alvin's daily commute from his home in Aurora to his school takes him by many city sights, including McNichols. "My friends on the reservation, they've got two or three kids. They've got labor jobs that are not going anywhere. My plan is not to go back to the reservation at all."

Like any rural village, Towaoc lacks opportunity, a term that goes beyond the simple question of jobs. There are no stores, no restaurants and few choices of employment beyond the tribe. Entertainment is cable TV, basketball in the gym or, often, drinking. There are 480 jobs on the reservation with 1,700 people. The unemployment rate is over 50 percent. People under twenty-five make up the majority of the population.

In Alvin's 1983 high school graduating class of a dozen Utes, most remain in Towaoc, working for the tribe. The reservation is a powerful cultural magnet, a lure that is both healthy and deadly for young Utes. The reservation is a cultural womb, where foods, faces and religious practices are familiar. But it can also stifle initiative. "The atmosphere is the same," said Alvin. "There's always going to be lots of parties. I'd end up with nothing to do. That's when you get restless."

Alvin played sports in Cortez and had many white friends, which helps him adjust in Denver. He never gave much thought to life after high school until his mother pushed him out. Then he went through a restless period in which he drank and wrecked a truck. "Now I won't party when I'm driving."

Historically, the Ute Mountain Ute tribe was run by a strong leader who "took care of things," said Judy. Thanks to oil and gas revenues, that atmosphere prevailed with per capita payments. With royalties slipping, Judy is faced not only with creating jobs, but with changing attitudes, too. "We have to work on our people and tell them that knowing something is not a disease."

A number of tribal enterprises have been created: a pottery shop employing thirty people, a weekend bingo operation employing twelve and the Weeminuche Construction Company, with sixty employees. The tribe itself employs 247 people but hires many white professionals to head departments.

Alvin worked for Weeminuche on several reservation jobs, including the construction of tribal headquarters and HUD homes. It is the most successful of the enterprises, but also the most criticized. The company is managed by a white-owned firm in Cortez, which receives 20 percent of the profits and returns another 10 percent to the tribe. Because it is tribally owned, it can get minority preference on jobs. In return, the managers are supposed to hire, train and promote Utes.

After five years, more than half of the employees are Ute, but they remain in the lowest labor jobs, which pay $7 to $12 an hour. "Our people aren't advancing," said Judy. "That's why we started the construction company, to give people the chance to learn a trade without leaving the reservation."

Rick Keck, Weeminuche's general manager, said most Utes he hires are starting from scratch. "Most of them have no experience. They didn't have jobs. They didn't have a mom or dad that got up and went to work." Many have drinking problems and fail to show up for work. Extra manpower must be figured into every job to cover for them.

Five Utes have advanced to machine operators, making $15 to $17 an hour, and eight are "becoming good carpenters," with pay up to $17 an hour. No Ute has reached management. Of fifteen foremen, two are Utes. Bob Frank, Judy's husband, who was a Washo tribal chairman in Nevada for sixteen years and ran his own construction company for eight, has been a foreman for Weeminuche. Keck said Judy's son, Alvin, could return as a foreman. "That's the goal— where tribal members are running things. But that's fifteen to twenty years away."

For now, Alvin hopes to overcome the pull of home. He shares a home in Denver with Sharon Quam, a Zuni Indian attending court-reporting school. Alvin will return to the reservation for the Sun Dance each July, but hopes to "nail down a pretty good job" in Denver.

"I try to keep a positive attitude—why I'm going to school and what I can accomplish by going to school. I've seen what you can do if you really want it. [But] you've got to know where you come from. I'm always going to be an Indian. It's inside, mostly in my heart."

15

"What Tribe Are You?"

*T*he run for Thanksgiving began at sunrise. The old blue van sped toward Cortez, traveling the full length of the mountain called the Sleeping Ute. By 7:30 A.M. it was racing back to Towaoc, reeking of roast turkey. "We've got enough food for 700 people," said Big Jim Knight, who drove thirty birds in his '58 Chevy panel truck. Another van behind him hauled ninety-six pumpkin pies, 1,000 rolls and a dozen relish trays to the plaza in the center of the reservation village.

"On the day before Thanksgiving we have a community meal for the tribe," said Jim, the son of Gladys Knight Hammond. "It's a tradition." The meal began at 11:00 A.M. in the dining hall, and by noon a line of Utes stretched out the steps, into the sunny plaza. As I waited in line, I realized that there aren't many meals we share with Native Americans. Foods, yes. They gave us corn, potatoes, peanuts, squash, wild rice, maple syrup and avocados. Thanksgiving without native food would be slim fare.

But we don't have many shared traditions that don't start with a treaty and end with a war. Thanksgiving is one. George Washington made Thanksgiving a national meal 200 years ago this month. But, as we all learn in school, the first Thanksgiving was in 1621 in Massachusetts, a three-day fall fete to celebrate the Pilgrim's survival through their first winter in the New World. It was very much an American feast: wild turkeys, clams, wild plums and cornbread. Invited Indians brought five deer.

The eastern tribes had taught the survivors of the *Mayflower* to plant corn, among other things. Squanto, an Algonquian, is said to have taught the trick of fertilizing the seed with dead fish.

Massasoit, chief of the Wampanoags, sat at the outdoor tables with the Pilgrims. Later his son, King Phillip, led the first widespread war against the encroaching white settlers in New England. After that, whites didn't give much thought to Indian largess or sharing a meal like this one.

Most of the Knights attended the community meal or helped dish food. Elders like Charlie moved to the front of the line.

"So what do you think of us Utes?" asked Gladys, out of the blue. She had fed me many times during my stay on the reservation. Just the night before, her kids had stewed up jerky and corn and baked oven bread in my honor. And her question was a fair one. I had posed many blunt ones to her.

"Well, I like you guys," I said. "I admire you."

She leaned away and gave me this look. "What does that mean, white man?"

It meant affection and respect—toward the Knights, toward the Utes and, through them, toward Indian culture. It meant also that 368 years after the first Thanksgiving celebrated native know-how, Indians still had much to teach me. History, for one. The Indian side is rarely told. The Knights helped me learn a bit of theirs. As contemporary as they are, the family has a sense of who they are and where they came from.

"What tribe are you?" Terry had asked me on our first meeting three months ago. It was a question meant to put me in an Indian frame of mind, and it succeeded.

Last week I got another lesson when Terry saddled up a horse named Thunder and we rode out past his father's house to a half-wild horse herd near Mesa Verde. The Utes were among the first Indians to adopt horses from the Spaniards, and their horsemanship still is a matter of pride. As we rode, Terry pointed to mounds around us, littered with pottery shards, Anasazi homesites. The Utes had left them undisturbed when they moved to the land around Ute Mountain.

In the herd was a colt that Charlie wanted to brand. Terry set the horses running across the dry and weedy plateau, while Thunder and I galloped ahead to flank them at the corral. The sun was setting behind the toe of Ute Mountain, and we moved like history across the land. Far more than I could ever grasp, the Knights have a sense of place and past.

Before anyone ate, Terry said a prayer in Ute, and the long line began to inch forward. Tribal employees filled plates of corn and beans, turkey and ham, dressing, potatoes, rolls and pie. People sat at tables in family groups. I sat across from Charlie, who sat next to Terry. I asked him what he had said in his prayer.

"Thank you!" he grinned, with a mouthful of food. "Thank you for the turkeys." I laughed, too, and put away my notebook.

As we emptied our plates, Charlie leaned back and grabbed his stomach, squeezing it over his belt. "Full," he said. He was dressed to kill in a beaded bolo, beaver hat and his corduroy jacket.

"You come back in the spring. Break colt." He waved his fingers between us, then held the reins of a bucking colt. "You, me. Break colt."

I asked when exactly.

"April, maybe March."

I chuckled. He was expressing Indian time. The Utes do not believe that time is money. Time is wisdom, and that can't be bought. Spending time in conversation with Charlie was a rich reward for me. Just like standing in line for the communal meal. It was another lesson learned from the Utes.

As I prepared to leave the reservation, I felt that I had come to know the Knights pretty well. But I knew I could not speak for them. When I told Judy Knight of invitations I had received to speak about the Utes, she said: "So, you've become an Indian expert?"

I have not. But I have become a proselytizer with one message: The Indians in our midst cannot be ignored. To do so only diminishes us. For me, traveling to the Ute Mountain Ute Reservation was like visiting a friendly foreign country with its own language, culture, religion and history. I came away enriched, broadened and appreciative of a people who have survived and are striving to maintain their integrity in a changing world.

I hoped they could continue to resist assimilation and not become just like us, in some American melting pot. That would be like dumping a Thanksgiving meal into a blender. The joy of Thanksgiving comes from the variety of flavors and textures, separate and distinct, that combine to create an American feast. So it is with our cultures.

That year, Thanksgiving for me was a quiet celebration of our differences. I'm glad I could share it with my Native American friends.

10/9.75

11/97 8